The Trauma-Informed School

A Step-by-Step Implementation Guide for Administrators and School Personnel

BOOKS BY HEATHER T. FORBES, LCSW

Help for Billy

Beyond Consequences, Logic, and Control: Volume 1

Beyond Consequences, Logic, and Control: Volume 1
Spanish Edition

Beyond Consequences, Logic, and Control: Volume 1
Russian Edition

Beyond Consequences, Logic, and Control: Volume 2

Dare to Love

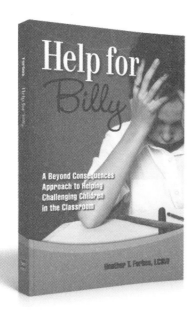

OTHER BOOKS BY JIM SPORLEDER
AND HEATHER T. FORBES, LCSW

A Study Guide for Help for Billy

www.help-for-billy.com

The Trauma-Informed School

A Step-by-Step Implementation Guide for Administrators and School Personnel

Jim Sporleder

and

Heather T. Forbes, LCSW

Beyond Consequences Institute, LLC

BOULDER, COLORADO

The Trauma-Informed School

A Step-by-Step Implementation Guide for Administrators and School Personnel

Published by:
Beyond Consequences Institute, LLC
www.BeyondConsequences.com

ISBN: 978-0-9978501-5-4

Cover Design & Layout:
Mimi Emeline
Emeline Design
www. emelinedesign.com

Contents

PART THREE: STRATEGIES

APPENDIX

For the most up-to-date and electronic versions of forms in the Appendix, visit:
www.TheTraumaInformedSchool.com/appendix

ENDNOTES

Foreword

———————————◼———————————

When we arrived in Walla Walla, Washington the summer of 2012 to scout out the location for what would become the acclaimed documentary, *Paper Tigers*, we were struck by the contrast of the prosperous wine industry juxtaposed to the older dilapidated neighborhoods. Surrounding us were buildings in desperate need of repair, including our destination, Lincoln Alternative High School.

It was hard to imagine that this old, somewhat barren building was where groundbreaking approaches to helping traumatized children had taken flight. As we climbed the stairs, Principal Jim Sporleder stood waiting at the door. With a John Wayne drawl, it wasn't hard to picture Jim as the imposing disciplinarian he was for many years. But then came Jim's warm smile and gentle handshake that reminded us of a man who was completely the opposite.

After all, we'd read his story in numerous articles. Jim had completely reformed the struggling Lincoln High Alternative High School. It was a change in thinking that ignited Jim's shift and it came from the message of the landmark Adverse Childhood Experiences Study that showed that a childhood of neglect and abuse alters the brains and bodies of children. As Jim began to understand that childhood experiences create learning difficulties and behavioral challenges, he realized his students weren't "bad kids." They were kids whose unfortunate childhoods had hard-wired them for conflict and primal survival, leaving them unable to navigate the demands of higher education.

This all explained why Lincoln was plagued with gang fights in the halls, chaotic classrooms, truancy, drugs, and arrests. By all accounts, implementing a trauma-informed approach in a school such as Lincoln High was an administrative suicide mission.

Yet for Jim, taking the science and converting it to best practices came naturally and with great success. However, it wasn't the increase in test scores and graduation rates that inspired our decision to spend an entire year in Walla Walla making *Paper Tigers*, it was from a chance encounter with a student that set the course for this decision.

Through a chance encounter, we witnessed a student at the school who had multicolored hair, piercings, and tattoos. Everything about this young man screamed, "keep away." But as this encounter unfolded, we saw Jim embrace him with a big bear hug and the hardened teen crumbled into a boy needing love. And there it was, beyond the science, that we saw firsthand the healing power of love and compassion.

The guide you are about to read contains the hard-learned lessons from a principal's journey of moving a school from barely surviving to thriving. Additionally, it weaves in the experience and mental-health perspective from Heather T. Forbes, LCSW, one of the top trauma experts in this field.

Their combined work in this masterpiece will support you in successfully implementing a trauma-informed model. It is beyond comprehensive. In the following pages, you will have everything you need from an overview of trauma to detailed checklists to specific strategies, and much, much more.

This complete and informative guide is one-of-a-kind. It will give you the valuable answers you are seeking for your school. This guide will truly answer the ultimate question that is sweeping the educational field and that is, "What does a trauma-informed school look like?"

The answers await you right here!

James Redford
Director
KPJR Films

Karen Pritzker
Executive Producer
KPJR Films

PART ONE

Toxic Stress and Its Relationship to Learning

CHAPTER ONE

Introduction

You and your staff are about to begin a journey that will not only be transforming for your students, but for you too. You will be inspired and forever changed by witnessing the resiliency and hope students exhibit from having a strong connection with a caring adult. It is our most challenging students that are truly our gifts. They are the ones who move us to a higher order of understanding the true meaning of unconditional love and they are the ones who will bring us to our highest potential. Get ready for a hard but amazing journey!

Trauma—Students who have been impacted by trauma carry a very heavy load and operate at a continual high level of stress. For most, their trauma wasn't a one time incident...it didn't happen overnight. It happened and continues to happen on a perpetual and long-term basis. Many of our students experienced years of toxic stress in toxic home environments that shifted them into living every moment of everyday in survival mode. Their new "normal" is fear, reactivity, and failure. This is how they have survived. It is all they know. The result is that their brains are wired for fear...their brains are not "bad" and their reactivity isn't necessarily "wrong." They are products of their environments. They have survival brains and that's how they enter their classrooms everyday.

This is a brain issue, not a behavioral issue. Thus, change won't happen overnight. Change and healing for our most challenging of students will always be a process...it will take time.

When implementing a trauma-informed model in your school, the shift from a fear-based culture to a relationship-based and love-based

"The caretaker is the adult responsible for healthy brain development."

culture will also take time. Getting school staff and teachers to change how they think, act, and respond to students will take conscious effort and dedicated mindfulness. As staff and teachers make the shift, students will then follow suit and feel the shift in school culture as well. Students will begin to feel safer. They'll feel a greater sense of respect. They'll feel like somebody actually cares. They'll feel like they belong. The exciting news is that all of this will eventually result in lowered disciplinary reports and higher academic test scores.

The key to any type of change is to be consistent in all interactions with all students. This includes everyone at the school: administrators, office staff, paraeducators, guidance counselors, cafeteria workers, janitors, bus drivers, and, of course, classroom teachers. Creating a school-wide trauma-informed culture requires a shift from everyone, not just a few. The success of such a shift requires the collective whole.

There is no perfect model of a trauma-informed school without its own unforeseen challenges. As these challenges come up, the best advice the authors can give you is to trust in yourself. When you learn to make decisions out of love instead of fear, you will never be misguided. The answers will come when you are looking through the lens of trauma and unconditional love.

It is amazing that what our students do and the issues they bring to us are actually perfectly logical. We must recognize, however, that the logic they use is stemming from their perspective of fear, stress, and overwhelm. When we can get into their shoes, understand why they are doing the things they do, the answers and the solutions become very obvious. Solutions and answers also come from you trusting in your own strengths and gifts and staying open to seeing the dynamics in an objective and inquisitive manner.

"Punishment can't create or model those qualities we want in a child."
—America's Cradle to Prison Pipeline Report Children's Defense Fund

From the Top Down—As the administrator, you become the starting point—the catalyst—for the change to a trauma-informed school and this change begins in the main office. The main office is Ground Zero. It becomes the model for others to witness and experience what a trauma-informed environment is all about.

The main office is the foundation for the implementation process. All members of the front office must work as a team and support one another with this new paradigm shift until it becomes a normal part of how business is conducted at your school. Modeling in the front office of what it means to be a trauma-informed school will give teachers confidence in implementing their own strategies in their classrooms. It will affirm them in their efforts and will serve as a teaching ground.

Additionally, your best feedback is the feedback students share with their teachers. They will begin to mention to their teachers that something feels different and new, in the main office. They may not be able to put words to it, but when you create a family climate in your school, your students will undoubtedly notice the shift. They will experience being treated with respect and with the feeling of being valued. Word will spread like wildfire.

Consistency is the key. Repetitive experiences of being treated with dignity, respect, and a sense of "I matter," will change students for the better. Even those who express resistance at first, will come around in time after they see the shift happening to the other students in the school. But it will take being consistent and creating an unconditional environment that demonstrates love and forgiveness while at the same time holds strong boundaries and expectations.

Trauma-impacted students are going to have their difficult days; you need to stay consistent in your approach and style. It also requires holding students accountable for their behavior. These will be teachable moments and a wonderful time to start building your own caring adult relationships with your students. Students will respond in their own time, some will respond sooner than others. It is important that you keep in mind that students' reactions are not personal; some students have greater trust issues and have learned to operate in "survival mode."

It takes time for students to know what their triggers are and to learn strategies to self-regulate and manage their stress. What you will begin to notice rather quickly however, is that if you take time with students to listen, to validate their stress levels, and to seek the causes of their behaviors, you will begin to develop a caring adult relationship that will only get stronger over time. In turn, this will result in the student demonstrating more appropriate behaviors and being more motivated due to the influence you have over this student, not the control that we traditionally thought would be the variable to make this happen.

The main office staff must commit to the implementation strategies given in this guide. If you have one office staff member who is not buying into the new model, he or she can do more damage than good. It's important to know that many of us have our own backgrounds of trauma that are unresolved. The best way to understand someone who resists, is through one main concept: resistance is fear. We will explore strategies on how to support and guide this type of resistance in Chapter 6.

"When the adult is not able to stay regulated when approaching a student who is dysregulated, the outcome will be to escalate the student to their breaking point."

All for One and One for All—The trauma-informed model works for all students—everyone benefits from being treated with kindness and connecting to caring staff. The trauma-informed model becomes a part of your everyday practice. It is not a model that is used to distinguish which students might be trauma-impacted or not. All K-12 students benefit from this approach and all will thrive. The reality is this, if it works with our most challenging students, certainly it will work with our less challenging ones.

The students with whom you may be having the greatest impact are the ones who may not actually respond well to your kindness–you just never know. This is a powerful reminder to seek out those students who isolate, disrupt, or have attendance issues. Make sure to acknowledge them and let them know you are happy to see them in school.

You won't have 100 percent success but you can love all your students 100 percent unconditionally. Healing occurs through each caring adult relationship that you can place in the student's village of support.

"Many students who are labeled as manipulating and wanting attention, are students who are seeking connection."

– Avis Smith/ Head Smart Trauma Start

Implementation 101– The following chapters are designed to give you all the details and specific steps you will need to take to create a trauma-informed school. However, to give you a sneak-preview of what it takes, here is a list of the five critical steps needed to accomplish this goal. Take a look at these steps and know that the details and the "how-to's" are waiting for you in the following pages. Trust that when all five are implemented, you'll be on the cutting edge and you will have accomplished this amazing goal!

"The brain drives behavior."

THE FIVE CRITICAL STEPS TO IMPLEMENTING A TRAUMA-INFORMED SCHOOL

	CONCEPT	MANTRA	STRATEGY
1	The stress is coming from outside of school.	*It's not about me.*	Drop your personal mirror.
2	Allow the student to de-escalate and regulate before solving the issue at hand.	*Problem solving and solutions can't be worked through while "in the moment."*	Designate a quiet place(s) where students can feel safe to de-escalate.
3	It's never about the issue at hand. It goes much deeper.	*What's really driving this child's behavior?*	Be the one who listens and values the student's voice… ask how you can help. Explore the underlying issue behind the behavior.
4	It's a brain issue, not a behavioral issue.	*My job is to help this student regulate, not simply behave.*	Incorporate regulatory activities into the culture of the classroom and support students in their ability to learn how to self-regulate.
5	Discipline is to teach, not to punish.	*Discipline should happen through the context of relationship.*	Use consequences that keep students in school and foster the building of trust and safety with caring adults.

"From Surviving to Thriving"
LINCOLN HIGH SCHOOL
BY JIM SPORLEDER

In the spring of 2010, I attended a training on complex trauma with John Medina and I knew at that moment that we had to change how we dealt with and interacted with our students. As principal of Lincoln High School (an alternative school) in Walla Walla, Washington, we were dealing with students who were constantly needing to be disciplined. I was hit with a lighting bolt at this training: these students acted the way they did because of the trauma they had endured in the past or because of the current trauma they were going home to every night.

"The single greatest predictor of academic success that exists is the emotional stability of the home. It's not the classroom. And if you really wanted to do educational reform, you would start with the home." John Medina

I realized that we couldn't expect our students to focus at school after they'd been abused the night before. So, we developed and implemented a trauma-informed model at Lincoln. Despite it being our first try and not being perfect, it worked! We had an increase in attendance. We had students making up credits in areas where they were deficient. The bottom line was that as we addressed the social/emotional needs of the students and once the relationships were built, the data came naturally. And I believe it all happened because of what our students found—and that was hope.

It was the hope and resilience that re-engaged our students back into the learning environment. It was all about the hope—the hope was huge. The hope was the catalyst. Once hope was re-established through the trauma-informed environment where relationships became the priority, then test scores improved dramatically and graduation rates increased. We definitely focused on academics but we had to first focus on the social and emotional needs of our students in order to get to the academics. It is about creating balance between all of it.

As a nation, we are data driven in our policies and funding for schools. Yet in reality, when we focus on the data the actual increase is minimal. The research is now showing that teachers today are working harder than they've ever worked yet we are getting very little improvement in our academic scores.

Our disciplinary referrals decreased, our graduation rates increased, and our test scores improved drastically because we were creating a balance of it all:

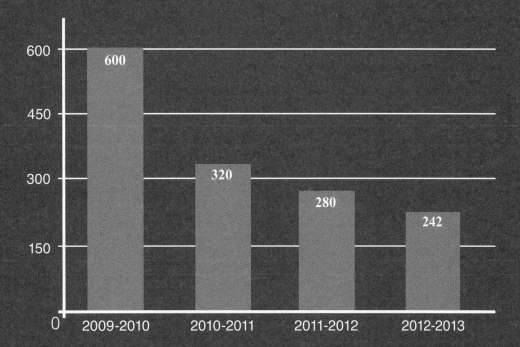

STUDENT DISCIPLINARY OFFICE REFERRALS

SCHOOL INCIDENTS REQUIRING POLICE ACTION

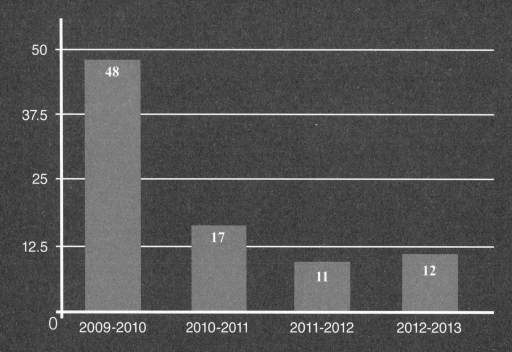

NUMBER OF DAYS STUDENTS WERE OUT OF SCHOOL

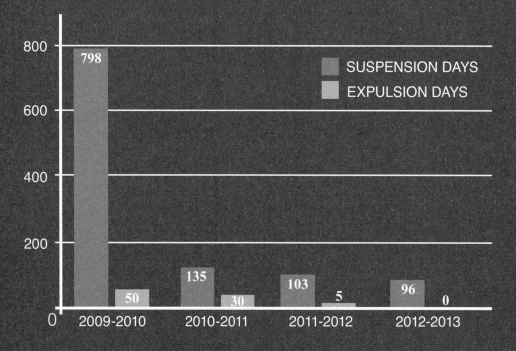

LINCOLN HIGH SCHOOL GRADUATION RATES
"does not include 5th year graduates"

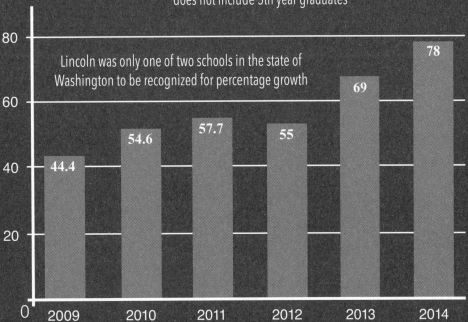

Lincoln was only one of two schools in the state of
Washington to be recognized for percentage growth

44.4	54.6	57.7	55	69	78
2009	2010	2011	2012	2013	2014

STATE ASSESSMENT SCORES 2012 & 2013

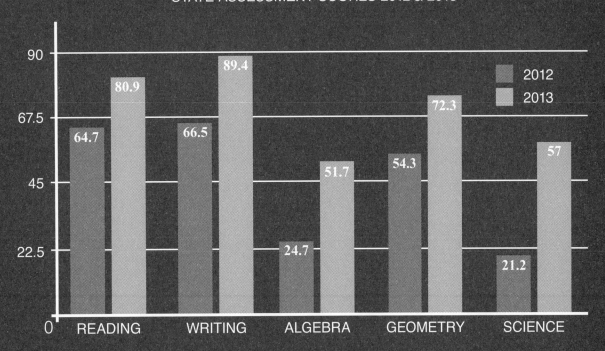

	READING	WRITING	ALGEBRA	GEOMETRY	SCIENCE
2012	64.7	66.5	24.7	54.3	21.2
2013	80.9	89.4	51.7	72.3	57

This data shows we can get where we want to go, we just have to change our approach.

Also, we didn't give homework. Our kids didn't have a quiet place to go home to and do homework. What we did was increase their day as far as classes. Our students were taking seven periods a day instead of six. So the students coming in who were deficient in credits started seeing themselves catch up. They could catch up on two credits per year in addition to going to summer school. They started to see themselves catching up and realized they could graduate.

I would bring new students in my office and say, "We won't be giving you homework, but here's the trade off: we expect you to work hard in all your classes—bell to bell. So when you leave here, you can say you've worked your tail off."

CHAPTER TWO

Adverse Childhood Experiences

The Adverse Childhood Experiences Study (ACE Study) is an ongoing research study conducted through the collaboration of Kaiser Permanente and the Centers for Disease Control and Prevention. The study shows a direct correlation between adverse childhood experiences (ACEs) and health and social problems as an adult.

ACEs are defined as some of the most intensive and frequently occurring sources of stress that children (from birth to 18) might suffer in life. These range from physical, emotional or sexual abuse, neglect, witnessing violence in the home, living with alcohol and/or substance abuser, and community violence.

> *"There is a direct link between childhood trauma and adult onset of chronic disease, as well as mental illness, doing time in prison, and work issues, such as absenteeism."*
> — *Jane Ellen Stevens*

The Basics of the ACE Study—The demographics of the ACE study were as follows:

- 17,300 adults were part of the original study that is still active today

- 75% were Caucasian

- 39% were college graduates

- 36% had some college background

- All participants have/had livable wages and health insurance

- All were middle class or affluent

"Chronic childhood trauma—such as being regularly slapped or punched, constantly belittled and berated, living with a parent who's alcoholic or depressed—releases a constant flood of stress hormones that damage the structure and function of a child's developing brain."

— Jane Ellen Stevens

The ACE Study has been active for more than twenty years. It was started by Dr. Vincent Felitti. He took a compassionate approach to wondering why his successful obesity program, offered by his employer, Kaiser Permanente, was seeing a significant number of patients dropping out of the program after experiencing high success of losing massive amounts of weight. Dr. Felitti's concern for his patients led him to start looking into his patient's personal histories who had left his program. He came up with some compelling commonalities. The patients that were dropping out of the program showed a pattern of experiencing abuse and neglect as children.

In 1992, Felitti teamed up with Dr. Robert Anda, who had taken a particular interest in Felitti's unusual findings on account of his own related work for the Centers for Disease Control and Prevention. The pair then embarked on what would become a landmark research effort: the Adverse Childhood Experiences Study. More than 50 scientific articles have been written on the study and hundreds of conferences and workshops have been held to discuss the work.

The 10 Adverse Childhood Experiences—We know that there are more than the 10 ACE's that came out in the ACE Study, but these are the top 10 ACE's that surfaced and were most common within the 17,300 participants. The ACE's are grouped into two categories:

1. Childhood Maltreatment & Neglect
2. Dysfunctional Family Environment

The following is the list of ACE's used in the study:

1. SEXUAL ABUSE: Any act of a sexual nature, which uses the child for the sexual gratification of the adult, including rape, molestation, prostitution, pornography, or other form of sexual exploitation of children.

2. PHYSICAL ABUSE: Generally defined as any non-accidental physical injury to the child including striking, kicking, burning, or biting the child, or any action that results in a physical impairment or harms the child's health and welfare.

3. EMOTIONAL ABUSE: Defined as emotional or psychological injury to the child as evidenced by a substantial change in behavior, emotional response or

anxiety, depression, withdrawal, or aggressive behavior.

4. PHYSICAL NEGLECT: Defined as the failure of a parent or other person with responsibility for the child to provide needed food, clothing, shelter, education, medical care, or supervision such that the child's health, safety, and well-being are threatened with harm.

5. EMOTIONAL NEGLECT: Defined as the failure of a parent to provide needed emotional attention, support, recognition, love, and empathic response such that the child's emotional health and development are threatened with harm.

6. LOSS OF A PARENT: The discontinuation of contact with a parent due to death, divorce, or abandonment.

7. WITNESSING FAMILY VIOLENCE: Being a witness to violence creates significant emotional and psychological damage due to the high stress experienced by the child.

8. INCARCERATION OF A FAMILY MEMBER: The experience of having any family member in jail can create substantial emotional issues, such as grief and loss, stigmatization, anxiety, and depression.

9. HAVING A MENTALLY ILL, DEPRESSED, OR SUICIDAL FAMILY MEMBER: Growing up in a family dealing with mental health issues can cause confusion, fear, anxiety, stress, lack of attention, and concern regarding the child's own emotional health.

10. LIVING WITH A DRUG ADDICTED OR ALCOHOLIC FAMILY MEMBER: Drug and alcohol addiction of parents can negatively impact a child's sense of safety, predictability, stability, normalcy, connectedness, and attachment.

"More adverse childhood experiences result in a higher risk of medical, mental and social problems as an adult."
– Jane Ellen Stevens

If you want to test yourself, simply give yourself one point for each of the above ACE's that you have experienced from birth to 18 years of age. Add them up and you have your ACE Score.

ACE Score: _____

An ACE score of 6 is predicted to take 20 years off of your life expectancy with no caring adult intervention.

The ACE Pyramid—The ACE Pyramid represents the idea that the ACE Study works from a whole-life perspective. Working from this framework, it shows how adverse childhood experiences (ACE's) are directly correlated to the increase in risk factors for disease and a person's emotional and social well-being through their lifespan.

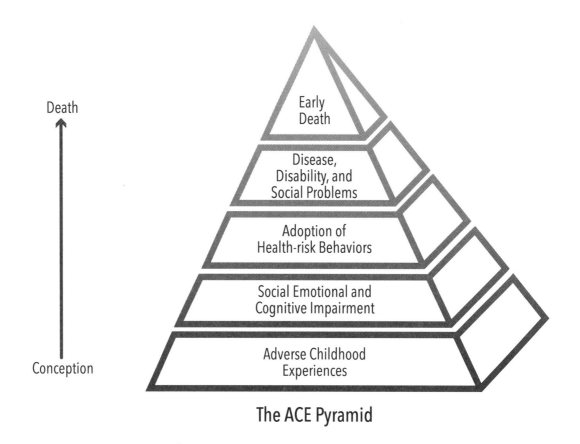

The ACE Pyramid

The significance of the ACE Study as it relates to schools is that children who are exposed to multiple ACEs are overloaded with stress hormones, which leaves them in a constant state of survival. This makes the absorption of new academic material much more challenging and puts these students in a difficult place to handle rules and authority figures. These are the students who are stressed-out, overwhelmed, unable to focus, and emotionally on edge. In other words these are the students we have traditionally labeled as the "problem students" or the "disruptive students."

A study out of Washington State University demonstrated that students who had at least three ACEs were three times likelier to experience academic failures. They were also five times as likely to have attendance issues and six times as likely to exhibit behavioral problems.[1] Thus, the ACEs study should provide the foundation for making a paradigm shift in the manner in which we approach our students.

We are living in one of the most stressful times in human history and this is having an impact on our children and youth. The level of stressful experiences many of our students go through even before they enter into their academic careers is on the rise. Their brains are wired for fear and their perception of how they fit into the world is fear-based. We can no longer ask our students to change to fit their environment because it simply isn't working. It is time to change the environment to fit our students.

Andy vs. Billy—Making the shift to a trauma-informed paradigm is critical because our schools were traditionally designed for children with low ACEs. The student with a low ACEs score is the student who has grown up in a loving, nurturing, stable, and predictable home with positive and emotionally secure experiences. This is the student we will refer to as "Andy." Andy begins his* academic career ready to learn. Andy's early childhood experiences have prepared Andy to be able to focus, learn, and stay attentive. Andy has a well-developed regulatory system and can handle the stress and demands of the academic environment. Andy's natural love for learning is intact and Andy's sense of curiosity is ever expanding.

"Children with toxic stress live much of their lives in fight, flight or fright (freeze) mode. They respond to the world as a place of constant danger."
— *Jane Ellen Stevens*

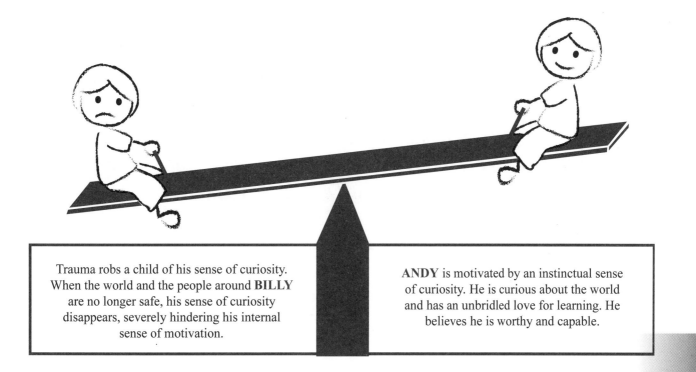

Trauma robs a child of his sense of curiosity. When the world and the people around **BILLY** are no longer safe, his sense of curiosity disappears, severely hindering his internal sense of motivation.

ANDY is motivated by an instinctual sense of curiosity. He is curious about the world and has an unbridled love for learning. He believes he is worthy and capable.

"Billy," on the other hand, is the student we will refer to as the student who has a high ACEs score. Billy is the student who has had adverse childhood experiences in the past or presently, or both. Billy is the student who shows up to school in a high stress state, unable to focus, and unmotivated. Billy is the student who either overreacts to small and inconsequential situations or completely shuts down and disconnects from what is going on around him.* Billy is the student who continues to challenge a school's disciplinary policies as he not only doesn't respond positively to punishment but he continues to get worse. Additionally, Billy is the student who doesn't even respond to positive reward systems. They too seem to only keep Billy spiraling downward.

Billy is the reason we as a collective academic society are being challenged to rethink the "way we've always done it" in the past. And more importantly, Billy is the student who is challenging each one of us to rethink the meaning of relationship, connection, and love. Billy is the student who will move each one of us to a higher order of love.

"Well, imagine you're walking in the forest and you see a bear... your heart starts to pound, your pupils dilate, your airways open up, and you are ready to either fight that bear or run from the bear. And that is wonderful if you're in a forest and there's a bear. But the problem is what happens when the bear comes home every night and this system is activated over and over and over again, and it goes from being adaptive, or life-saving, to maladaptive, or health-damaging. Children are especially sensitive to this repeated stress activation, because their brains and bodies are just developing. High doses of adversity not only affect brain structure and function, they affect the developing immune system, developing hormonal systems, and even the way our DNA is read and transcribed."
— *Dr. Nadine Burke Harris, Center for Youth Wellness*

* Throughout this guide, "Andy" and "Billy" are referred to as masculine or in the masculine tense in order to avoid clumsy construction. However, Andy and Billy can be either male or female.

"I Need Water"
CHEROKEE SCHOOL
BY HEATHER T. FORBES, LCSW

I was walking by the courtyard on a hot and humid Florida morning when the 2nd grade class was out for recess. I noticed my client, Billy, with his class but the teacher was looking very frustrated with him. I walked out to see if I could offer any assistance. Billy was hot, sweaty, and very agitated. He was sounding like a broken record, "I need water. I need water. I need water."

In response, the teacher told Billy, "You'll get water once you get in line with the rest of the class." Billy's response to this was, "I need water. I need water."

The teacher then held up her clipboard with her pen and said, "Billy, I'm going to take points off your point chart unless you get into line right now." Billy's response to this was, "I need water. I need water."

I immediately knew this was far greater than Billy being noncompliant. I had read Billy's file. At two years old, Billy was found walking down the red light district in Orlando by himself at 2:00 a.m. He was hungry and severely dehydrated when the police found him.

Connecting the dots of this earlier traumatic experience (even though it was six years ago) with the incident unfolding in front of me, I asked the teacher if I could take Billy with me and get him off her hands. In her dysregulated and frustrated state, she said, "Yes, take him!"

I went up to Billy and said, "You're going to be okay. Let's get you some water. You're going to make it." Trauma has no time-line and in that moment, Billy was back being that two-years old: lost, scared, and thirsty. He was in a fear state so I met him in that fear state with empathy, reassurance, and safety. He walked in with me to the water fountain and I offered him the water, free of a lecture about having to behave or a review of how he has to follow the rules. He drank the water. I had him step aside with me and I worked him through taking some deep breaths, reassuring him he was safe and that he was going to be okay.

This only took a few minutes and by the time Billy was back to a state of regulation, the teacher and the rest of his class was finished getting their water, lined up about to head back to class. I looked at Billy and asked if he was ready to go back with his class and he said, "Yes, Miss Heather. I'm okay." I gave him that look of, "Yes, you are and you can make it the rest of the day. I know you can!"

I went back and checked in on him at the end of the school day. His teacher said he had been "great" and that he had made it through the entire afternoon without a single point being taken off his point chart, a rare occurrence.

CHAPTER THREE

Trauma, Stress, and the Brain

Trauma is defined by the American Psychological Association (APA) as "an emotional response to a terrible event like an accident, rape or natural disaster." The problem with this definition is that it only includes a description of the event, rather than the experience one has with the event. In other words, trauma is really the experience or perception of the event that leaves one feeling hopeless, helpless, or powerless.

It isn't the event itself that defines whether an event is traumatic or not. It is the FEELING that the event creates. It has been shown that when a traumatic event happens in a child's life while there is a caring, calm, and confident adult connected to the child, it is far less traumatic than when the event occurs without such a connection.

With this understanding, trauma can include a wide range of experiences, not just an accident, rape, or natural disaster as defined by the APA. A child falling off his bike while out in the woods all alone, feeling like he is going to die, can be trauma. To relate to the traumatic experiences our students have had, we must be willing to expand our view and definition of what constitutes trauma.

Trauma defined: "Overwhelming demands placed upon the physiological system that result in a profound of vulnerability and/or loss of of control."
— *R.D. Macy*

Complex Trauma—Complex trauma is trauma on steroids. It is "the experience of multiple or chronic and prolonged, developmentally adverse traumatic events, most often of a personal nature (e.g., sexual or physical abuse, war, community violence) and early-life onset. These exposures often occur within the child's caregiving system." [1]

The ACEs study shows that if a child experiences at least one ACE, he will most likely experience another ACE. For example, 81% of the participants who reported growing up with household substance abuse, experienced an additional ACE. For the entire population of the study, it was shown that 81% to 98% of those who reported one ACE also reported a least one additional ACE. This means that most of our students who have experienced one type of trauma have or are experiencing multiple other types of trauma.

Toxic Stress—When children have prolonged experiences of adversity without a caring adult in their lives, the result is toxic stress. Their bodies remain in activation mode (fight-flight-freeze). Stress activates the body's physiological response with increased levels of stress hormones. Normally, higher levels of stress hormones are essential for our survival. However, excessive exposure to stress is harmful because the body continues to pump out high levels of stress hormones which then become toxic to the human body. The cumulative result of this over-activated stress-response system in the context of chronic adversity is what is known as toxic stress.

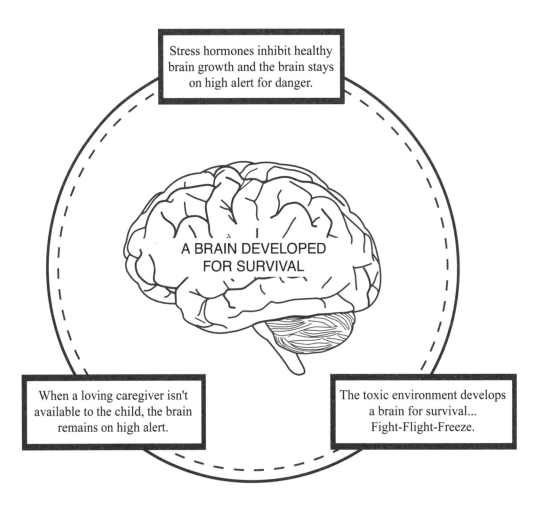

The negative effects of toxic stress for an adult are bad but for a child like Billy whose body system is still developing and growing under these conditions, the effects are exponentially worse. Toxic stress can physically, emotionally, socially, academically, and cognitively hinder the developing child. Most children coming out of toxic environments will show signs of developmental deficits and, unfortunately, this can easily be misinterpreted as "bad" or "negative" behavior.

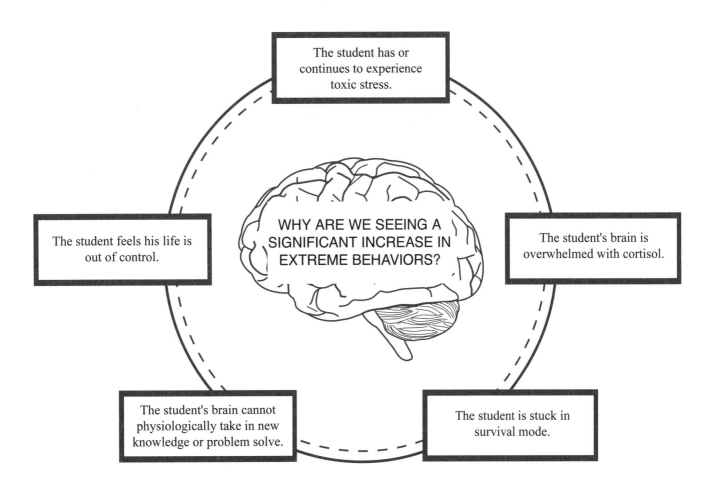

Research from Harvard states, "Adverse environments resulting from neglect, abuse, and/or exposure to violence can impair the development of executive function skills as a result of the disruptive effects of toxic stress on the developing architecture of the brain. Chaotic (and thus, from the child's standpoint, unpredictable) environments can also lead to poor self-regulatory behaviors and impulse control."[2]

IMPORTANT FACTS TO UNDESTANDING
A STUDENT IMPACTED BY TRAUMA

- The child's caregiver is responsible for the brain development of the child from birth to 18 years of age.

- Neuroscience tells us that the "brain drives behavior."

- There is a story behind every behavior…we know that students with survival brains have two common factors behind their behavior: feeling unsafe and fear of failure.

- The strategies for working with students impacted by trauma are effective strategies for all students (both our Billys and our Andys).

- We cannot assume that trauma impacted students come prepared emotionally or socially when they enter our schools. The source of their inner pain has been caused by the adult caregivers and/or their environments.

Top-Down vs. Bottom-Up—The difference in the brain of a child who grows up in a healthy environment, a.k.a. Andy, is remarkably different from the child who grows up in a stressful environment, a.k.a., Billy. Andy has had safe and predictable experiences which have hardwired Andy's brain with more capacity to successfully function in an academic environment.

For a student with healthy brain development, the neocortex has control over the survival impulses of the lower two parts of the brain. The student is able to control his brain from the top down. The neocortex keeps the brain in check and can control the limbic system which is the center for our emotions. With a healthy and regulated brain, the neocortex also controls the reptilian brain, which is one of the oldest parts of the brain. It is located at the top of the brain stem, with its main job being that of survival when it comes upon danger.

"The amygdala in the emotional center sees and hears everything that occurs to us instantaneously and is the trigger point for the fight or flight response."
– Daniel Goldman

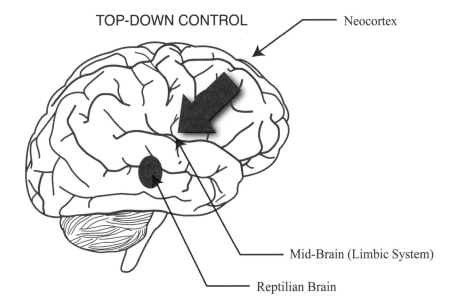

TOP-DOWN CONTROL

Neocortex

Mid-Brain (Limbic System)

Reptilian Brain

When a student is living under high amounts of stress or has had an intense history of trauma, this top-down control system fails and the lower parts of the brain become more dominate. Decisions for students like Billy are made from a bottom-up control system instead.

In this bottom-up control system whereby the mid-brain is in charge, life happens in the next fifteen seconds...there is no future and there is no past. If Billy wants something, it doesn't matter if there is a consequence that afternoon because the concept of time is nonexistent in this part of the brain. This explains why students who are dysregulated are functioning from the part of their brain where there is no reason, no connection to consequences, and no care for anyone but themselves.

"90% of life is about remaining calm."
– Dr. Chris Feudtner

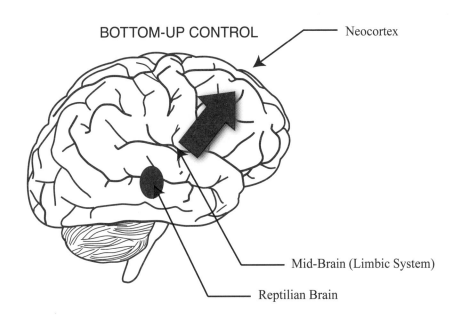

BOTTOM-UP CONTROL

Neocortex

Mid-Brain (Limbic System)

Reptilian Brain

Language is processed in the left brain of the neocortex so when a student like Billy is working from a bottom-up control, he can easily get irritated with too much talking because the words are not making sense to him and it is only getting him more stressed out. This is also why teachers find themselves overwhelmed when trying to reason with a student like Billy, because it appears as if Billy simply isn't listening. In reality, it is more like talking to a lizard when a student is deep in the lower states of the brain.

"The behavior is not about you...it's about the student and what's going on in their lives."

-Jim Sporleder

When putting this information into the context of the academic environment, it makes sense why disruptive students are typically struggling academically. They physiologically cannot learn when they are functioning from a bottom-up control system. Their ability to access their logical thinking, sequential thinking, memory storage and retrieval, auditory processing, language processing, and organizing is compromised as these are all functions of the neocortex.

With this understanding of how the brain operates, surely we are called to re-examine how we have been perceiving disruptive students. We have been judging and labeling these students as "troubled" or "bad" when the truth is, they physiologically cannot make appropriate decisions or calm themselves when they are functioning from a bottom-up control. They are in survival; their brains are flooded with the stress hormone, cortisol.

Andy's Brain vs. Billy's Brain—Early childhood experiences greatly influence how a child's brain develops. The impact of these early years reaches far beyond just the preschool years. Comparing the brains of our Andys with our Billys, provides clarity and insight into why their behaviors are so drastically different.

ANDY: Andy's consistent and predictable life has fostered the development of his executive functions. One of the most important aspects of his brain development is his working memory. He has the ability to remember. Andy has the capacity to hold and manipulate information over short periods of time. He can store information but more importantly, he can retrieve this information...his memory recall is intact. He has the ability to remember multiple thoughts and directives. There is space for more than one thought which gives him the ability to complete one task and then immediately remember the next task waiting in the queue.

Andy's brain has the ability to plan and organize and scores in the normal to high range in his intellectual and cognitive functioning. Andy's visual-spatial and perceptual-organizational skills are strong which make it easy for him to excel in the academic environment, free of struggles and challenges. He has the ability to focus, concentrate, and pay attention. He can focus on a task without daydreaming or becoming easily distracted.

Andy has inhibitory control which means he has impulse control. Simply, he has brakes. He has self-control and persistence. Andy also understands cause and effect, because he has the ability to think in linear terms combined with the ability to implement sequential thinking. His ability to think beyond the obvious allows him to identify main ideas and to think outside the box.

Andy also has mental flexibility which affords him the ability to get back on task after being interrupted. This mental flexibility allows him to understand multiple meanings and nebulous concepts. He can easily recognize mistakes and fix them, with the ability to move on to the next task without getting stuck. He has problem solving skills that can be applied to a variety of situations and challenges.

Andy's brain is wired to succeed in the academic environment.

BILLY: Billy's brain is much more rigid and underdeveloped compared to Andy's. The trauma has slowed down his brain development. Billy is likely to have some speech, language, motor, sensory, learning, and processing deficits. Typically, Billy struggles with not just one, but multiple deficits in these areas as a result of the complex trauma.

Billy struggles to sustain focus, pay attention, and process information adequately in the traditional academic environment. Billy does better in a multi-sensory environment that includes more than just auditory instruction. Billy becomes easily confused and frustrated with only verbal instruction because of his auditory attention and auditory-sequential memory deficits. He has difficulties in his ability to organize incoming verbal material while maintaining clear and connected thoughts. In other words, he gets confused and scattered very easily.

Billy typically has challenges in terms of attention, reasoning, and decision making. He is highly sensitive to distractions or any interfering task. He is limited in his ability to recall simple factual

"When working with trauma-impacted students, we must reach their hearts before we can reach their heads."
– Dr. Ken Ginsburg

information, understand abstractive logic, and comprehend verbal reasoning. Billy gets overwhelmed easily which can result in impulsivity and the lack of ability to rapidly and efficiently process academic information. He then struggles to keep up with the academic demands and often acts out in response to these deficits.

This acting out is also a result of Billy's inability to problem solve adequately. His brain is wired in a rigid and concrete fashion which makes it difficult to understand multiple perspectives and multiple outcomes. His abstractive reasoning skills are underdeveloped. He is literal in his interpretation of language and cannot see outside the box. There are no gray areas of understanding. It is either black or white, good or bad, right or wrong.

Billy typically shows impairment in memory. He is weak in his ability to retain, encode, and recall newly presented information. Billy requires an environment with multi-sensory teaching techniques to process and store information efficiently and effectively.

Billy lacks the ability to connect socially outside of a structured academic environment and typically demonstrates high anxiety, insecurity, and operates from a fear-based platform. Billy has a deep fear of failure and does not trust adults. His mantra is, "Adults are not to be trusted" because adults have caused him deep pain.

HEALTHY VS UNHEALTHY BRAIN	
HEALTHY BRAIN (ANDY)	**UNHEALTHY BRAIN (BILLY)**
• Has the ability to be kind and compassionate.	• Is impulsive, angry, and frustrated.
• Is able to think rationally.	• Can't process consequences.
• Is able to show empathy and understanding.	• Is highly stressed.
• Has self-awareness.	• Thinks from an emotional platform and is irrational.
• Has the ability to be imaginative and think logically.	• Struggles with memory and focusing.
• Has a sense of curiosity because it feels safe.	• Can't process sequentially so school rewards don't make any sense.
• Can process language readily.	• Only understands the moment—now. There is no future there is no past.
• Has a sense of time (past, present, future).	
• Uses higher order thinking skills.	• Becomes more stressed out with traditional disciplinary techniques.
• Is controlled by the neocortex with a "top-down" control system intact.	• Is controlled by the lower brain with a "bottom-up" control system intact.

The Solution— We must help to calm their brains and return our students back to a top-down control. Fear-based punishment, logic, and control are not the mechanisms to do this. Relationship, connection, and acceptance are the only way. These are the students who need safe and caring adult relationships to help them move from a bottom-up control back up to a top-down control, where learning can take place.

If our students are functioning with a bottom-up control system, it is physiologically impossible for them to function appropriately and constructively in the classroom or on the playground. It is up to us as adults to understand the power of relationships. If we stay regulated when the student is dysregulated, then we are at the critical moment to help the student come back to calm and to bring a sense of safety to the student and their school surroundings. They are not out to get us; they want connection but live in too much fear to do it on their own. We must teach them strategies that help them build their self-regulatory skills and demonstrate that we value their voice and feelings.

"Thanks for Listening"

LINCOLN HIGH SCHOOL
BY JIM SPORLEDER

When I got to Lincoln, there was a blatant disregard for anybody in authority—it was just rampant. Everything was "F-you!"

"Billy, why are you late to class?" "F-you!"

"Billy, can you please take your feet off the desk?" "F-you!"

"Billy, could you please take your headphones off?" "F-you!"

"Billy, where are you going?" "F-you!"

"Good morning, Billy." "F-you!"

The consequence for this type of language was an automatic three-day suspension because in the traditional thinking, "Kids can't talk to adults that way." Then one day I decided it was time to try something different. Instead of an out-of-school suspension, I was giving a student an in-school suspension for dropping the F-bomb at school.

My mind was made up to make the paradigm shift but my body was having a different reaction. I was literally sick to my stomach...I was completely nauseous. But I held strong to our motto of going from reacting and telling to asking and responding.

Through the physical discomfort, I kept it simple and said, "Billy, this doesn't sound like you. What's going on?" He said, "I'm so pissed off today!" Instead of giving him the lecture of why he can't use the F-word even if he is pissed off, I sat back and agreed with him, "Yeah, I can see that." And then he immediately opened up to it all, "Sporleder, my dad is a drunk. He's let me down all my life. When I was a little kid he was going to come pick me up but he never showed up. He hasn't shown up for anything. I'm just SO pissed off!"

As I watched and listened to him download all his disappointment, anger, and stress, all I could think about was how much this must hurt. He settled for a minute and then got to the root of the issue of what had put him to his breaking point this particular day. He said, "I'm 16 today and he promised me a car. I thought it was the one thing he was going to follow through on. But he let me down again and I came to school so pissed off!" As he de-escalated and with all his heart he looked at me and said, "Sporleder, Terry didn't deserve for me to tell him to F-off. I really need to apologize."

Even with him taking ownership and responsibility for his actions, he still needed to go to in-school suspension. Before he left to go to the ISS room, he said to me, "Sporleder, thanks for talking with me. I feel so much better." But the irony was that I didn't talk to him; I just listened, acknowledged what he was going through, and accepted him.

After school, he went down and apologized to Terry on his own.

CHAPTER FOUR

Why We Need a New Approach

Zero Tolerance Policy—In the mid 1990's, the United States Congress, along with several states, passed laws with the intention of reducing violence, notably gun violence, in schools. The laws not only encouraged harsh punishments but in many cases, mandated them. Following the implementation of these laws, there was a rise in out-of-school suspensions and expulsions. Many of these out-of-school suspensions and expulsions were given for mundane and non-violent infractions. The unfortunate fall-out for our most behaviorally challenged students was lost educational opportunities and the labeling of them as delinquents and criminals. Additionally, two decades of research showed no evidence that removing students from school improved school safety or student behavior.

These zero tolerance policies are the least trauma-informed policies ever put into practice in our schools. They ignore the mental and emotional needs of the most vulnerable of students in our schools and allow absolutely no understanding to the individual needs of students. Ironically, the students who need the most help are punished, judged, and pushed away. This only works to deepen their trauma related issues. This zero tolerance policy is actually a zero relationship policy.

"If the only tool you have is a hammer, you tend to see every problem as a nail."
– Abraham Maslow

School-to-Prison Pipeline—Harsh disciplinary polices that remove students from the classroom typically shift the "burden" of these students to the juvenile justice system and it is being done at alarming rates. Dubbed the "school-to-prison pipeline," these harsh policies encourage police presence at schools, and use punitive and fear-based tactics that include physical restraint and arresting students within the schools.

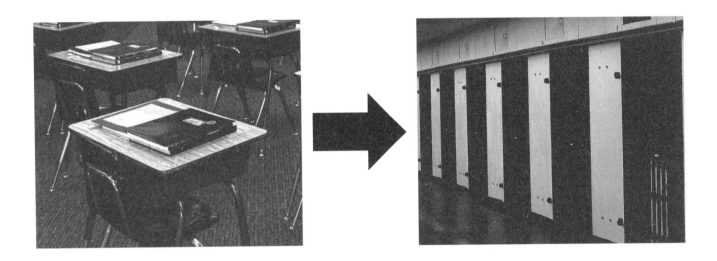

Two groups of students who are disproportionately represented in the school-to-prison pipeline are racial minorities and students with disabilities. According to the U.S. Department of Education Office for Civil Rights, when compared to white students, African-American students are 3.5 times more likely to be suspended or expelled. African-American students account for 18 percent of students in our schools yet they represent 46 present of those suspended more than one time.

For students with disabilities, the numbers are equally troubling. One report found that while 8.6 percent of public school children have been identified as having disabilities that affect their ability to learn, these students make up 32 percent of youth in juvenile detention centers.

The Way We've Always Done It—Trauma research is telling us that our traditional practices don't work. Yet, we are hesitant to let go of the way we have been trained. We are hesitant to step away to make the changes necessary to meet the needs of ALL of our students.

CHAPTER FOUR | 33

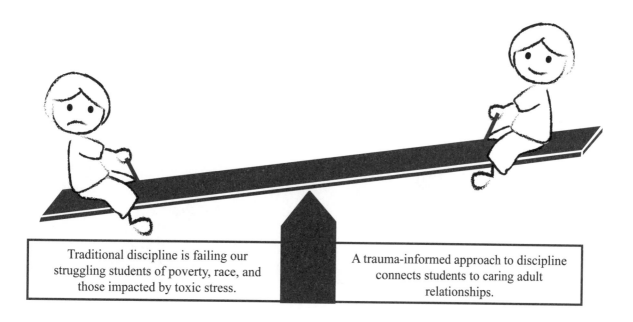

Traditional discipline is failing our struggling students of poverty, race, and those impacted by toxic stress.

A trauma-informed approach to discipline connects students to caring adult relationships.

If we are willing to use the science as the catalyst for changing our approach to school discipline within the entire culture of the school, improvements in behavior and academic performance are possible.

THE TRADITIONAL CYCLE OF TRAUMA IN OUR SCHOOLS

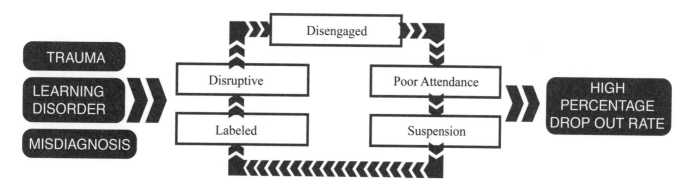

What is "Trauma-Informed?"—Trauma-informed refers to all of the ways in which a service system is influenced by having an understanding of trauma and the ways in which it is modified to be responsive to the impact of traumatic stress. A program that is "trauma-informed operates within a model or framework that incorporates an understanding of the ways in which trauma impacts an individual's socio-emotional health. This framework should theoretically, decrease the risk of re-traumatization, as well as contribute more generally to recovery from traumatic stress." [1]

A trauma-informed school meets the needs of ALL students, both our Andys and our Billys.

> **Students who have survival brains do not have cause and effect thinking so they struggle with consequences. Their toxic environments have not prepared them for predictable outcomes as the events in their lives have been unpredictable. This explains why these students struggle with consequences and fail in an environment that is based on reward and punishment.**

A trauma-informed school focuses first on relationship and second on discipline. The reality is that the more a child has a relationship with at least one trusting adult, the less acting out this student will have in the classroom. We as a human species are designed to be in relationships. We are biologically designed to be in community. We are more regulated, happier, and healthier when we are connected.

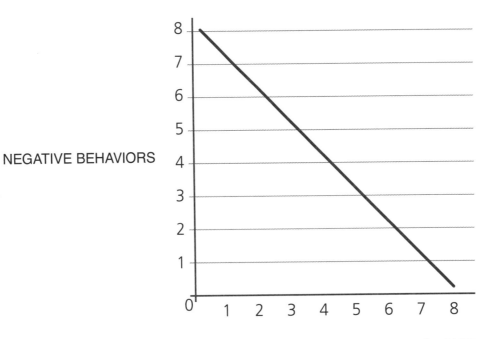

NEGATIVE BEHAVIORS

STRENGTH OF STUDENT'S RELATIONSHIP
WITH A CARING ADULT

Trauma research tells us that students who survive trauma and grow to be successful identify one single variable in their success: they were connected to a caring adult who believed in them and cared about them. Teachers are the most frequently endorsed adults who make a powerful impact on children's and adolescent's direction in life.

Our bodies are designed to react in a fight-flight-freeze mode as a protection device when we are in danger. This adrenalin rush (cortisol) is meant to last five to eight minutes for us to make a quick decision for our safety. Students of trauma experience high levels of cortisol in their brains and it is with them all the time, 24/7. This is the reason that trauma has such an impact on brain development. When students are highly escalated, they are working from the stem of their brains and physically not able to engage in the learning for fear of failure or feeling unsafe. They are, as mentioned in Chapter 2, in a bottom-up control system.

"Many of our schools are good schools if only this were 1965."
— Louise Stoll and Dean Fink

WHY WE NEED A TRAUMA-INFORMED APPROACH

They are in fight-flight-freeze mode.

They have no social cues or awareness of expected behavior.

They are grossly ill-equipped to handle stress and trauma.

They will need a nurturing adult to calm their nervous systems.

They will fail in school and in life without learning to properly deal with stress.

Trauma-informed strategies help students feel safe and to become regulated. This happens when the student connects with an adult and is able to trust the adult for their safety and security. We have such a powerful opportunity to build caring adult relationships with these struggling students, many of whom have no one to turn to in their lives for support in the home! It is critical that we understand the significant impact each one of us has on our students. For some, it may take time to build the trust with the adult, but for others it can come quicker.

The time you spend today with a student has the potential to have a profound effect on the student for a life-time.

"Creating a trauma-informed school isn't about teachers becoming therapists. It's about creating an environment that focuses on relationship, trust, and emotional safety."
— *Heather T. Forbes, LCSW*

A caring adult relationship is foundational in helping students impacted by trauma…it helps them move from hopelessness to HOPE. We have the ability to change students' life paths and help them gain the resiliency they need to overcome their adverse childhood experiences.

Hierarchy of Learning—Children have a natural love for learning, yet what we as a collective society have forgotten is that children are first emotional beings. They operate at an emotional level, not an intellectual level. That's the definition of being a child.

A survey was created by the Beyond Consequences Institute (BCI) to ask the opinions of students regarding what they needed at school to make learning better. The survey was completed by students from first to twelfth grade and their answers gave profound insight into the needs of students. Only 2% of the students made suggestions regarding actual academic improvements. The remaining answers focused on suggestions to meet their social and emotional needs.

The students' responses centered on identifying ways the school could meet their physiological needs, safety concerns, relationship needs, and self-esteem needs. The collective responses from all the students created a similar framework to psychologist Abraham Maslow's hierarchy of needs theory. Maslow suggested that the needs of individuals must be met before they will have a strong desire for improving themselves and moving forward in their growth. In order of priority, Maslow theorized that individuals must have their physiological, safety, love/belonging/and esteem needs met prior to being motivated at the self-actualization level. He also believed that when these basic needs are deficient in one's life, the feelings of being anxious and tense are typically present.

Taking this framework of human motivation developed by Maslow, the same basic principles can be applied directly to the student in the classroom. The "Hierarchy of Learning" pyramid describes why we need to have a trauma-informed approach in our schools.

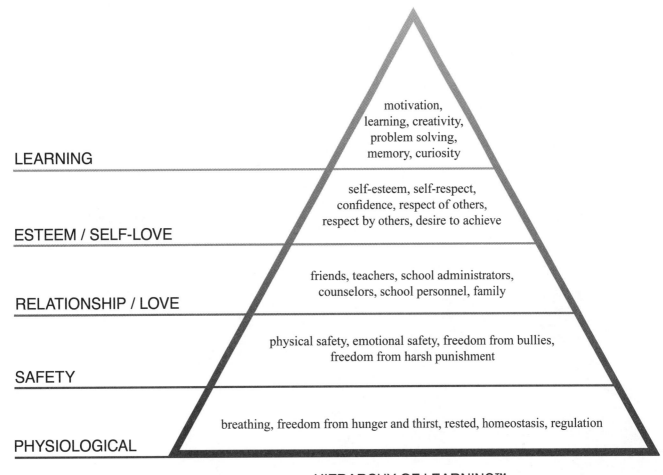

LEARNING

motivation, learning, creativity, problem solving, memory, curiosity

ESTEEM / SELF-LOVE

self-esteem, self-respect, confidence, respect of others, respect by others, desire to achieve

RELATIONSHIP / LOVE

friends, teachers, school administrators, counselors, school personnel, family

SAFETY

physical safety, emotional safety, freedom from bullies, freedom from harsh punishment

PHYSIOLOGICAL

breathing, freedom from hunger and thirst, rested, homeostasis, regulation

HIERARCHY OF LEARNING™

Instead of addressing the top of the pyramid, which is what we have traditionally done, we must first address everything below the top in order to ultimately reach the top of the pyramid. Trusting the process of meeting the social and emotional needs of our students to achieve high test-scores and successful graduation rates is the ultimate in making the shift to a trauma-informed school.

"Respect is a learned behavior and thus, so is disrespect. You act the way you've been treated."

– *Heather T. Forbes, LCSW*

"Here's a Glass of Water"

LINCOLN HIGH SCHOOL
BY JIM SPORLEDER

Billy was in class and students were making comments about her boyfriend. They relentlessly kept talking about him and she was overhearing the whole conversation. Finally, when class dismissed, Billy waited outside for two of the main girls instigating the conversation. One of the girls didn't want anything to do with her and left. However, when Billy confronted the other girl saying, "What's with you talking about my boyfriend?", the girl told Billy to "Shut the F-up!"

Billy just lost it at that moment and went after her. She started pounding on her and assaulting her. We had it on camera. It was an extremely aggressive fight that Billy initiated.

When Billy was brought into the office, she was given a glass of water and we talked to her very respectfully. She was given a chance to calm down. Billy knew she shouldn't have done what she did and took full ownership for her reactivity. She was very insightful. She admitted that she should have come and talked to someone prior to the incident and that she knew there were people at the school who were available to her.

We still had to charge her for the assault, but because she was so cooperative, I let her know we weren't going to handcuff her to take her in. The School Resource Officer (SRO) came in and processed with her everything that was going to happen. Before they took her in to JJC, the SRO expressed his appreciation for her cooperation. He repeated that he would not handcuff her, but she was still going to have to go through the whole court regarding the assault.

The SRO's message to her was, "It is my job to keep you safe and to keep the school safe for everyone. But it can be done with respect and cooperation, which I am appreciative of how you've been able to do this with me today."

When Billy retells this story today, she always expresses how the simple offer of a glass of water and the kindness she received when she was brought into the office changed everything about how she was able to face the consequences of her actions. This level of kindness and respect, even though she was "guilty" of the assault, changed how Billy was able to move forward.

Three years after this incident, I attended Billy's graduation from Lincoln. Billy graduated with several scholarships and will be attending community college.

CHAPTER FIVE

Resilience

The American Psychological Association defines resilience as the process of adapting well in the face of adversity, trauma, tragedy, threats or significant sources of stress—such as family and relationship problems. Or as the cliché puts it more succinctly, what doesn't kill you makes you stronger.

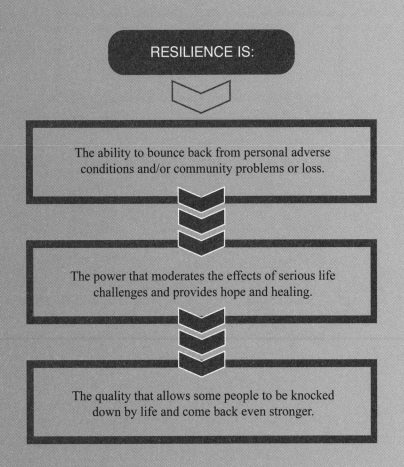

RESILIENCE IS:

The ability to bounce back from personal adverse conditions and/or community problems or loss.

The power that moderates the effects of serious life challenges and provides hope and healing.

The quality that allows some people to be knocked down by life and come back even stronger.

"However long the night, the dawn will break."
- African Proverb

Trauma requires those impacted by it to dig deep—deep within the caverns of their heart to find and uncover the resilience that will sustain them through their intense challenges. Resilience affords them the ability to overcome and rise from the ashes. Ultimately, it is resiliency that moves them from a place of surviving, to a place of thriving on a life journey of fulfillment, meaning, and purpose.

"We cannot live only for ourselves. A thousand fibers connect us with our fellow men; and among those fibers, as sympathetic threads, our actions run as causes, and they come back to us as effects."

- Herman Melville

Two of the main factors psychologists have identified that help someone find their resiliency is the ability to regulate emotions and optimism. Both of these are directly supported through the context of a strong, safe, and unconditional relationship. For our students impacted by trauma, the relationship we develop with them is the key factor in helping them to come through their challenges to stay in a place of hope, knowing that they matter and always have a "safe-base" to turn to when in need.

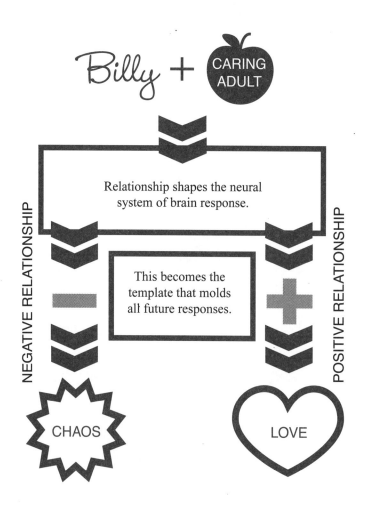

Billy + CARING ADULT

NEGATIVE RELATIONSHIP — POSITIVE RELATIONSHIP

Relationship shapes the neural system of brain response.

This becomes the template that molds all future responses.

CHAOS

LOVE

Protective Factors—Protective factors are resources, skills, strengths, and coping mechanisms available to those impacted by trauma to help them more effectively handle the stress and reduce the long-term effects of the trauma.

Protective factors can be divided up into two categories: external factors and internal factors. External factors include, as mentioned, caring and supportive relationships as well as a supportive and safe environment, challenging but obtainable expectations for success, and opportunities to belong and to have meaningful interactions with others. Internal factors include problem solving skills, competent and effective social skills, autonomy, sense of purpose, sense of "all-rightness," and a vision for a better future.

PROTECTIVE FACTORS THAT PROMOTE RESILIENCE	
EXTERNAL FACTORS	INTERNAL FACTORS
• Caring and supportive relationships • Supportive and safe environments • Challenging but obtainable expectations for success • Opportunities to belong • Opportunities to have meaningful interactions with others • Connection to community	• Competent and efficient social skills • Problem solving skills • Autonomy • Sense of purpose • Feelings of being effective • Sense of being "all right" • Vision of better future • Self-regulatory skills

This list of protective factors is not only essential for the Billys of our schools, they are also important for our Andys. Every student, whether impacted by trauma or not, stands to benefit from their academic environment providing more tools for sustainability with a focus on social and emotional development.

Before we can get our students prepared for learning, we have to focus on their wounds, understand their history of failures, and address their social and emotional development.

The importance of providing protective factors to our students can be seen in the figure below. Firstly, many of our students are developmentally too immature to have adequate internal tools at the individual level. Secondly, their families are too chaotic and unpredictable to provide the support they need (and in many cases, it is the family that is the source of the trauma). The next closest available system is the school for these students. Their school has to become their family; their school becomes the closest available support system to provide them the protective factors needed to find the resilience they need for long-term success. Additionally, we can draw on the community to help support our Billys as this is the next closest support system.

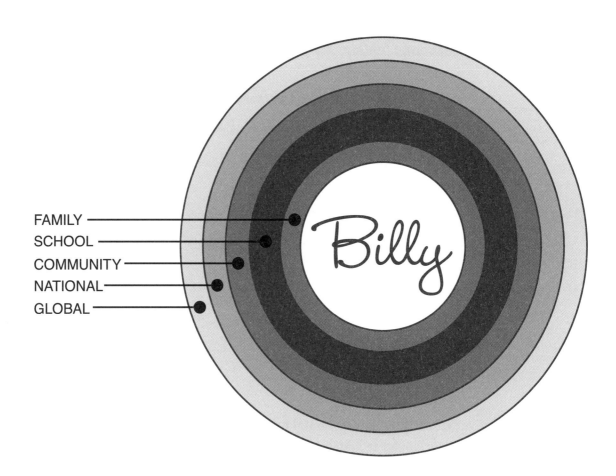

Skill Building—Children impacted by trauma have deficits in their ability to navigate in the world. Skills typically learned in the home environment were missed or taught in negative ways. Resiliency affords these students the opportunity to "redo" and "catch-up" on these skills in the school environment. Learning these life skills will prove as vital to these students as mastering academic concepts presented in the math, science, and English classes. The following is a list of many of the skills these students need in order to excel academically:

- Master the art of self-regulating.
- Attach to a caring adult.
- Develop self-esteem.
- Make appropriate choices.
- Take responsibility.
- Ask for help.
- Accept help.
- Show appreciation.
- Experience success.
- Learn to self-advocate.
- Trust themselves.
- Trust those in authority.
- Develop and maintain healthy friendships.
- Identify triggers that create reactivity and negative behaviors.
- Develop problem-solving skills.
- Show empathy.
- Express feelings.
- Acknowledge and own mistakes.
- Work as a cooperative team member.
- Adhere to rules and expectations.
- Meet expectations.
- Stay within established boundaries.
- Accept consequences gracefully.
- Give back to others.
- Help others.
- Develop self-control.
- Develop decision-making capabilities.
- Develop communication skills.
- Make eye-contact.
- Learn to listen.
- Speak logically.

"Most of us can read the writing on the wall; we just assume it's addressed to someone else."
—*Ivern Ball*

"If you think you can do a thing or think you can't do a thing, you're right."
—*Henry Ford*

• Deepen language skills.

• Use appropriate language when frustrated and upset.

Every student deserves to become the person he or she is meant to be. Building resilience in the classroom by supporting and connecting with the Billys in our schools will move them from a place of pain, stress, and overwhelm to healing, hope, and graduation!

More information and resources on resilience can be found at:

Michael Unger, PhD: www.michaelungar.com

WhyTry Resilience Education: www.whytry.org

"Killing the Pain with Pot"

LINCOLN HIGH SCHOOL
BY JIM SPORLEDER

We got a phone call that some students were smoking pot in one of the allies so I radioed for my SRO to pull them back in. Three of our students were there and all three were high. When we got them back to school, we divided them up and talked to them individually. The student I was talking to was new to Lincoln. Here's how the dialogue unfolded:

Me: "Hey, I'm not judging you. But I can tell just by looking at your face that you're using very heavily. On a scale of one to ten, where is your stress right now?"

Billy: "I'm at a 10

Me: "Wow! That's way too heavy of a burden for anyone to carry. No one can function when they're at a ten. The brain just isn't in a position to function. You don't have to answer me, but are you smoking in the morning before you come to school?"

Billy: "Yes."

Me: "Are you smoking at lunch every day?"

Billy: "Yes."

Me: "Are you smoking in the evenings every day?"

Billy: "Yes."

Me: "That explains how much of a burden you have. Something in your life is happening that is causing that much usage. You don't have to tell me but I can tell you're dealing with a heavy burden."

Billy: "I can't smoke enough to make the thoughts leave my head."

Me: "What thoughts are going through your head?"

Billy: "I lost my sister in a house fire. And she was the only one who didn't get out. I feel like I should have been there. I would have run into the house and I would have done everything to save her."

Me: "Oh, Billy...to have to live with that."

Billy: "What haunts me everyday is that my little sister was in foster care and her foster father beat her to death. I wasn't there to protect her. I can't smoke enough to get that thought out of my mind. Its in my mind every day."

Me: "Can I help you? I'm not a professional counselor...I really feel like you need some support and someone to talk to that can professionally really help you. If you get that help."

Not everyone likes counseling but he took me up on the offer and we got him connected. The counseling changed Billy's life. His face cleared up, he was smiling, and he was becoming more outgoing.

I later pulled him aside and said, "Billy, you look so dang good! It isn't any of my business if you're using but it sure doesn't look like it." He said, "I'm not going to lie to you but I smoke about three times a month."

I think back and ask myself, "What if I had suspended this student for smoking pot and never asked the question, 'What's really going on here?'"

PART TWO

Implementing a Trauma-Informed School

CHAPTER SIX

Working as a Team

Being a trauma-informed school is cutting edge and the beginning of a journey in which you will never look back. There are three key elements to have in place prior to the full implementation process. These include the following:

- Administration
- Leadership Team
- Staff

"Alone we can do so little, together we can do so much."

– Helen Keller

KEY ELEMENTS TO HAVE IN PLACE PRIOR TO THE FULL IMPLEMENTATION PROCESS

ADMINISTRATION	LEADERSHIP TEAM	STAFF
It will take a 100% commitment from the school administration.	A leadership team that represents all of the staff needs to be created.	It will take the commitment of 75-80% of your staff.

Administration—To be successful in this journey, the administrative staff needs to be 100% committed. Effective change happens from a top-down system. If there is conflict at the administrative level, it will filter down to the teachers and staff which will undermine the entire effort.

"Remember, teamwork begins by building trust. And the only way to do that is to overcome our need for invulnerability."

– Patrick Lencioni

You will need to work with any resistant administrators at the educational level. The science behind the understanding of toxic stress can have a powerful influence on helping people change their perspective. Instead of this being just a "fluffy feel-good" model, this is a model based off of science with proven outcomes and proven success.

Fear must be removed from the administrator's role at the school. Leadership and hierarchy is ineffective when it involves fear. Instead, leadership and hierarchy are established through the influence of relationship. Keeping an "open-door" policy with teachers and staff is critical. The trauma-informed model works to support the Billys of the school and this same principle is needed between the administration and the staff.

When an administrator walks into a classroom the goal is for the teacher to feel supported, not threatened. If a teacher's stress increases due to the interaction or the observation from an administrator, all is lost. The Billys of the classroom will feel this stress and this stress will increase the negative cycling of it all.

Additionally, when teachers feel supported instead of slipping into a state of fear, teachers will have a larger capacity to problem solve and to find effective solutions. The administrator/teacher or administrator/staff relationship is as important as the teacher/student relationship.

Leadership Team—The glue that will hold all of this together in the beginning is the creation of a Leadership Team. This team should be created with staff who are excited about this paradigm shift and who are "all-in." Find your "champions" of the school; they'll stand out from the others.

The Leadership Team should consist of ten to twelve people at the school who are enthusiastic about making the shift to a trauma-informed school. Best practice would have this team consist of the principal, a teacher from each grade, behavioral intervention specialist(s), guidance counselor(s), office receptionist, and even some of your support staff such as a paraeducator, head of the cafeteria, or even the custodian. Getting a sample from all areas of your school will make this a more wholistic and effective approach. Ideally, this Leadership Team is created a year before the entire school changes to a trauma-informed platform. The team's mission is to spearhead this initiative, modeling to all the other staff what this "looks like" and what is in store for everyone the coming year.

THE LEADERSHIP TEAM

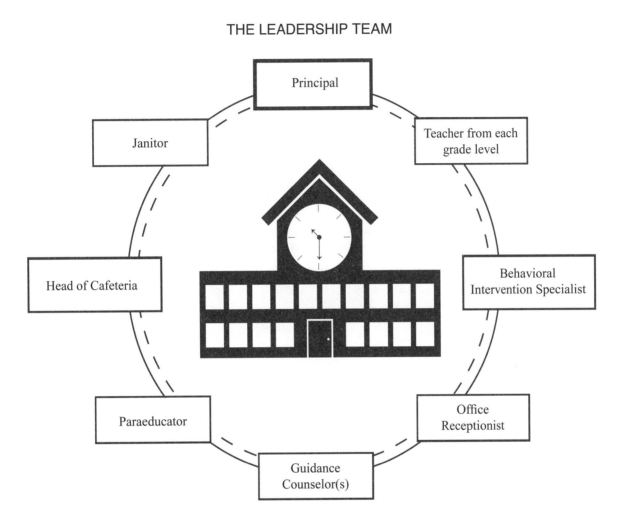

The Leadership Team is created the first year and becomes a tight-knit group. They all participate in a book study of *Help for Billy*, using the *Study Guide* as their curriculum. They spend time discussing how their interactions with students was modified from a behavioral focus to a trauma-relationship focus. They become the "go-to" people when challenging situations arise with students. They will be on call to provide a quick response to any situation, giving quick and responsive communication.

The principal serves as the head of the Leadership Team to keep the team learning, growing, and solidified. The principal can expect to have his/her role be that of a strong support and to be there when rough

AVAILABLE AT:
www.beyondconsequences.com

moments arise. And rough moments will arise, moments when it feels like it would be easier to go back to more traditional disciplinary methods.

Changing patterns in how we interact with students is hard work and when challenges present themselves, it is normal to feel like going back to the familiar is the best solution. However, this will be minimized with a strong team and with team members who feel like this information resonates with their soul. The more you work through difficult situations and as the interactions with students become more and more productive with this approach, the less you will experience any desire to return back to the old ways.

During the second year, the members of the Leadership Team then become mentors for the rest of the staff. These team members will lead small book study groups and use their expertise to guide and help other teachers during their beginning stages of switching to this model.

In both the first year and the years following, it might be necessary to bring in an outside consultant on some of your more challenging cases. A trauma-expert can lend a fresh eye and give advice from an objective perspective. As the old saying goes, "Sometimes you can't see the forest for the trees." Contact Jim Sporleder (www.sporlederconsulting.com) or the Beyond Consequences Institute (www.beyondconsequences. com) for more information.

Staff—During the second year, you will implement this model at an entire school level. Ideally, you want 100% of your staff on board. However, the reality is that this is typically not the case. You will have the "naysayers" and the resistant ones who will continue to see a student's negative behaviors as a matter of choice and who have a hard time letting go of traditional discipline. They tend to judge consequences by how much they hurt or punish, all of which is based off a punitive model.

Unfortunately, it can be difficult to move these individuals to a new understanding at first but it is suggested that you stay in constant and open conversation with them. Remember, resistance is fear. Use this model with them and support their resistance and look for their fear, treating them with dignity and respect. They need to feel like they have been heard. Many times, simply giving them a voice, hearing them out, and listening to their reasons for not being able to support a trauma-informed model is enough to help them start opening up to making the change. Connect with them just as you would a Billy in the school. Coach and support them.

"In order for the brain to comprehend, the heart must first listen."
— David Perkins

When in a conversation with a resistant staff member, simply listen. Don't listen to convince or listen to debate, just listen—that's the first step. Then, one of the most effective strategies you can have is to respond with questions. Below is a list of sample responses you can use, however, use your own style and what is most comfortable for you. And most of all, these responses need to come from your heart, not your head. This means that you are responding in a way to give the opposing staff member your patience, understanding, tolerance, and acceptance.

- "When you are stressed out, does it help you to have someone at that moment telling you not be upset and to make a better choice?"

- "When you are upset, what is more helpful, having someone just listen to you or having someone tell you what you should do?"

- "Let's look at this from a different angle. Why would we want to give the students what they want, because that is exactly what a day of suspension really is? It's a free day out of school, no school work, and on the streets unsupervised."

- "If we are going to hold our students accountable, don't we want to see them responsible for their attendance, for completing their school work, and for keeping up with their work?"

- "What would be the benefit of having a student out on the streets, unsupervised, as opposed to having them be in school, holding them accountable and supervised?"

- "Who was your favorite teacher in all of your academic career? Why was this person your favorite? (The answer is always because this person paid attention to them and got to know them.) Didn't you feel a deeper sense of motivation within yourself because of this person's interest in you?"

- "I agree that this model and paradigm shift is very hard. What do you need from me to support you with this transition?"

- "If you were in my position, what interventions would you be putting into place?" (Don't argue with the answer, just listen and notice the focus on behavior instead of regulation.)

- "We know what the research says about trauma-impacted students, how can we go back to a traditional model, when the research is telling us that it does not work?"

- "What research can you provide me to support a traditional model that would serve our students more effectively?"

"To go faster you must slow down."

– John Brunner

- "I believe that we are on the right path to serving our students most effectively; there is no turning back. How do you see me supporting you as we make this transition to better serve our students and families?"

- "Have you talked with any of your peers that have found this model helpful? What were their thoughts and insights?"

- "Would you like to problem solve some strategies that might make the implementation a smoother transition for you?"

- *When all efforts fail*: "Would you like me to advocate for you to transfer to a program that is more in line with your traditional beliefs?" (Have this discussion with your district administrator first.)

The good news is that many of the staff members showing signs of resistance at first will eventually come on board after they witness the changes and as a trauma-informed culture develops in your school. Sometimes it takes trusting the process. Change is hard. It is interesting that in some cases, however, those who were the most resistant can flip to the other side and soon become your greatest advocates for this model!

In the beginning, as long as you can get 75% to 80% of your staff to embrace this model and to have the willingness to change, that will be enough to get the momentum flowing. To determine which teachers make it into this majority, here is a checklist to use in your assessment of their readiness:

> *"If a child can't learn the way we teach, maybe we should teach the way they learn."*
> – *Ignacio Estrada*

- They understand that student learning and school success are impacted by ACEs and toxic stress when there are no interventions in place.

- They understand that they must drop their personal mirror. It's not about them…it's about what the student is going through.

- They accept that students cannot control their behavior when they are in the fight-flight-freeze mode.

- They understand that when students are under high levels of stress, their natural survival skill is to lash out in anger and fear. They understand that this has been how Billy has had to adjust to his toxic environment while trying to survive.

- They realize that a student's resistant, non-compliant, and disrespectful behavior is learned behavior.

- They agree that traditional discipline models do not work and that in-school suspensions need to be given as much as possible instead of suspending students from school.

- They realize that giving out-of-school suspensions is exactly what students want. They agree that rewarding these students with a free day out of school, not doing their classwork and instead on the streets of the community unsupervised is counterproductive.

- They are willing to try something new and demonstrate a willingness to be flexible in the process of learning a new model.

- They demonstrate an openness to being supported, corrected, and helped by the Leadership Team during the process of learning and implementing this model.

- They show a commitment to continuing the learning process by participating in a study group and/or support group with peers and other school staff.

"Really great people make you feel that you, too, can become great."

– Mark Twain

"Fight or Flight"
CHEROKEE SCHOOL
BY HEATHER T. FORBES, LCSW

Billy was seven years old and had a history of in utero drug exposure, sexual and physical abuse, witnessing domestic violence, and movement from multiple foster homes. He was diagnosed with ADHD, conduct disorder, PTSD, anxiety, and failure to thrive. Billy was also on a multiple number of high-powered medications. When he got dysregulated in the classroom, he would immediately go into fight or flight. There was minimal warning; he would either become violent or run out of the classroom.

One day I was walking in the hallway when the classes were in session and I saw Billy running out of his classroom. I had spent hours with him the previous months building a fairly strong relationship with him. He was approaching the front door and I knew I had to act fast. The school was located in downtown Orlando near a busy highway and if he ran out the door, it would truly be a safety issue that would be too far gone to be handled at the level of relationship.

I approached Billy gently and said, "Hey, Billy. Looks like you're having a hard time." He stopped, turned around, and looked at me. He couldn't even speak. He was too deep in his reptilian brain to access language. I calmly said, "Stay with me, Billy. You're not in trouble. I'm here to help."

I squatted down to his level and didn't say much more but I reached in my pocket and handed him a small box of raisins. I always kept raisins in my pocket, especially for him because I knew his history of not having enough food. Raisins were always a way to get him to calm down. He started eating the raisins and I was there breathing and staying present with him, not saying a word. When I could see he was calming down even further, I said, "I want to make sure you're safe. How about you come back to my office with me?" He didn't answer and I could see him still eyeing the front door, unsure of what to do. But he was close to coming with me. His body language was relaxing and he took a small step closer to me.

Just when I thought we were both going to head back to my office, another teacher who knew Billy and his history of running out of class, came out of her classroom. She saw Billy and yelled, "Billy, you can't be in the hallway! Get back to class now!"

In a split second, Billy went right back into fight or flight and bolted out of the front door. Just gone...gone out into traffic and now in danger. Staff was called out to chase Billy down and get him back into safety. And the cycle of running and being chased was once again playing out instead of being broken through relationship and understanding. So close....

It takes a community to wrap around our children; we all need to be on the same platform of understanding. Mixed messages are confusing to our students. They need all of us to be trauma-informed to be able to break the cycle of dysregulation that keeps them trapped and looped into chaos.

Creating a Calm Room

One of the hallmarks of a trauma-informed school that is drastically different from traditional schools is the philosophy of keeping children at school instead of sending them home when they become disruptive. This can be done by creating either a calm room or an in-school suspension room. Typically, the younger grades will have a calm room and the older grades can have an in-school suspension room (see Chapter 8 for an explanation of an in-school suspension room).

The use of a calm room focuses on helping students to regulate within the context of the relationship rather than leaving students to their own devices to regulate. It reflects the understanding that students' challenges are regulatory based, not behaviorally based. Before dissecting what it takes to create a calm room, an understanding of what happens to a child's sensory system needs to be taken into account.

"Everything you do can be done better from a place of relaxation."
– Stephen C. Paul

Sensory Processing Disorder—Due to the overwhelm experienced during trauma, a child's nervous system can be impacted whereby they become highly sensitive to sensory input. Their bodies have a difficult time processing and interpreting sensory signals. The result is a child who is in a state of neurological overdrive. Behavioral outbursts are common for these children, along with the inability to focus and sit still in the classroom. They can be highly anxious, have mood swings, and are easily overwhelmed in highly stimulating environments like the auditorium, the playground, or the cafeteria. These are also the children whose motor skills are challenged and may appear to be clumsy.

The clinical term for this is Sensory Processing Disorder (SPD). SPD is a spectrum disorder which means you'll have students who experience mild sensory symptoms as well as those who experience extreme symptoms. Children impacted by trauma have a greater possibility of exhibiting these symptoms, and it is important to remember that it affects aspects of their everyday life functions. It is chronic and it will certainly interrupt their academic performance if not recognized and addressed. Having a place for them to go to calm down is going to be imperative to their academic success.

Additionally, some schools may need to consider the possibility of having an occupational therapist available either part-time or full-time to help students with more pronounced sensory processing issues. Some Billys may need more one-on-one sensory-based work with an occupational therapist to improve their ability to perform the everyday requirements of an academic environment like interacting with friends, sustaining their regulation in over-stimulating environments such as the cafeteria and courtyard, and sitting and focusing on academic material.

Calm Room—As mentioned, the Billys of the school get easily overwhelmed (whether or not they have a diagnosis of SPD or not) which makes it difficult to have appropriate behavior in the classroom when they get overwhelmed. Taking breaks from the classroom environment can be one of the most helpful proactive ways to support these students.

Creating a "calm room" allows teachers to be able to have a place to send a student who is struggling in the classroom. It is a win-win scenario: the academics can continue in the classroom for all the other students yet Billy is also able to get the regulatory support he needs. Once Billy is regulated, he can then return to class ready to learn.

"Feelings are not supposed to be logical. Dangerous is the man who has rationalized his emotions."
– David Borenstein

THE MAKINGS OF A CALM ROOM—The Calm Room is supervised by a loving and nurturing individual who has been trained extensively in trauma. This person connects with the students to give them some one-on-one attention in order for them to calm down within the context of the relationship. This person works to cultivate and build a strong and trusting relationship with the Billys that find themselves frequenting this room.

When creating a Calm Room, consider including some of the regulatory objects listed on the following page:

- Bean bag chair

- Rocking chair

- A floor mat with pillows sectioned off in the room

- A swing

- Coloring books

- Play dough

- Fidget toys and stress balls

- Drawing and coloring supplies

- Stuffed animals

- Music with headphones

- Sand tray or rice tray

- Books

- Sensory bottles

- Bubbles to practice breathing

- Healthy snacks and water

- Lotion with calming scents

- A fish tank or bunnies

- Chewing gum (for oral sensory but supervised as needed)

- Soft blanket

- A "Sit and Spin"

"Just slow down. Slow down your speech. Slow down your breathing. Slow down your walking. Slow down your eating. And let this slower, steadier pace perfume your mind. Just slow down."

– Doko

ISOLATION VS. INTERACTION—While all the items listed above can be helpful to Billy, the most important element of this room is the interaction between the student and the Calm Room Supervisor. Simply having a child do a calming activity by themselves and then returning back to class is ineffective in the long run.

Remember one of the main objectives of a trauma-informed school is to help students learn how to regulate within the context of a relationship. These are students that have to learn how to trust adults for long-term success. They have to learn how to return back to their biological roots of being in connection with other human beings. Simply sitting in a corner and playing with play dough will not achieve this goal.

However, some students will become more dysregulated when the Calm Room Supervisor tries to interact with them. In these cases, it is best for the supervisor to take a few steps back to allow the student some space for emotional safety. If the student is playing with play dough, then the supervisor should play with play dough, joining the child in parallel play rather than interactive play.

Instead of the supervisor going back to his/her desk and ignoring the child completely, this solution gives the student the sense that this person is still with them but not in a close, intimate way that can feel too threatening to the student. Over time, the supervisor will find that he/she can move closer to this student until finally the student feels safe enough to interact and reciprocate in play. At this point, trust will have been built and the relationship will begin to solidify. It takes more time for some of your students due to a more severe traumatic history.

FENG SHUI—How the actual classroom is decorated also plays an important role. Consider using the following:

- Soft and warm colors
- A fan to block any outside noise such as street noise
- Incandescent lighting
- Fluorescent lighting panels
- Calming music (classical, drumming, soft jazz)

> *"Human beings are not meant to live alone. There is a fundamental biological imperative that propels you and every organism on this planet to be in a community, to be in relationship with other organisms."*
>
> *– Bruce H. Lipton*

SECLUSION NO MORE!—In the past, some schools have created calm rooms or recovery rooms that are no more than a padded room to lock children away in seclusion. This interpretation of a calm room is completely counterproductive to students needing to feel supported, accepted, and worthy. In the event a student becomes unsafe, these rooms should only be used as a last resort and ONLY when a regulated adult is in the room with the student. Additionally, they should only be used if the room is a full-size classroom, not a room the size of a walk-in closet.

Perhaps your first thought is that having an adult in the room with an aggressive child is putting the adult at risk. On the contrary. If the adult is relationship-based, regulated, and focusing on simply being in connection with the student instead of "making the student calm down and behave," the adult is no longer a threat to the student. In the past, adults got hurt because they were a threat to the student and were emotionally disconnected from the student.

The other reality is that if a student cannot be safe even with an adult who is regulated, the student simply should not be in school. This is a sign that the student needs a higher level of clinical mental health intervention.

"Just Be Their Friend"

CHEROKEE SCHOOL
BY HEATHER T. FORBES, LCSW

I was working for a community mental health agency that was doing clinical work in the Orange County (Florida) School District. I was one of the last hired for their school-based program and was assigned to Cherokee School. When I met the other school-based clinical staff and they found out I was assigned to this school, their reactions went something like this, "Oh my gawd! You're at Cherokee? That's the worst school in all of the district!" I knew I was in for a challenge.

Cherokee School was the "last-stop" kind of school. These were the students who were too much of a behavioral challenge to make it in the emotionally challenged programs at their home schools and for many students, this was at least their fourth or fifth school. It was elementary school-aged students and every classroom had a maximum of eight students with two adults in the classroom at every moment. Additionally, the school was staffed with several behavioral specialists who were available at a moment's notice to come to any classroom in the event of an unsafe event, which happened often.

The school worked from a deeply ingrained behavioral platform. Point charts, rewards, and time-outs were the norm. The previous clinical therapists who worked on campus like myself were armed with all sorts of traditional treatment approaches with complex treatment plans. None of their approaches worked from the platform of trauma.

When I started working with the students on my caseload, I knew it was much deeper than getting these children to think through their behaviors, to make better choices, or to sign behavioral contracts. I could see the fear—I mean the deep deep fear in their eyes. Their stories were heart wrenching and after doing some home visits, I knew the piece that was missing from their lives was the feeling of being safe and the knowing that they were special in this world. Their parents were unable to give them either.

So I threw out all the traditional therapeutic approaches. My "treatment plan" was simply to be a friend. I would work with the students, one-on-one in my quiet office and listen to their stories. I'd find out more about them. I'd offer an emotionally safe connection. I'd visit their families. I even visited one student's mother who was in the hospital for two weeks straight because he wasn't able to visit her and I'd report back to him how she was doing. This was my "clinical" work.

After being on campus for two months, the principal stopped me in the hallway and said "I don't know what interventions you're doing, but all the students on your caseload are showing a dramatic improvement!" I just smiled and thanked her while saying in my head, "I'm just being their friend. That's it. That's all they need!"

CHAPTER EIGHT

Creating an In-School Suspension Room

Traditionally, we have suspended students who have broken rules and are disruptive in the classroom. When students are suspended from school however, most times their parents are not home during the day which leaves them unsupervised at home or roaming the streets of the community and getting into more trouble. The other negative outcome of out-of-school suspension is that we miss the "teachable moment" in helping students to learn ways to better navigate academic and social situations when they get stressed-out and overwhelmed. In-school suspension (ISS) offers the opportunity for students to build stronger relationships at school, learn better coping skills, feel they are unconditionally accepted, and know that they belong.

The ISS should be flexible, structured, and play an important role in the trauma-informed approach. The goal of the ISS is to teach students how to do things differently next time. The goal is NOT to punish. Punishment only alienates students and keeps them in a negative cycle of dysregulation. To be effective, in-school suspensions should be in a dedicated room and every effort should be made to create this room as the safest place in the entire school. The ISS room will be the place where the most challenging of all your Billys will eventually find themselves and one of the first interventions for success is for them to feel physically safe and contained in a classroom that helps their nervous systems begin to settle.

"Each person holds so much power within themselves that needs to be let out. Sometimes they just need a little nudge, a little direction, a little support, a little coaching, and the greatest things can happen."
— *Pete Carroll*

ISS Supervisor—To be effective, the ISS room needs to be in a separate classroom, self-contained, and without outside distractions. It needs to be run by a professional with the following characteristics:

• The ISS supervisor needs to have a deep knowledge about trauma-informed practices.

• The ISS supervisor should have a natural ability to connect with students and demonstrate strong relationship building skills.

• The supervisor needs to organize the ISS room so that students can work without being distracted.

• The ISS supervisor should know that if the student is coming into ISS and he/she needs to process, it is okay to do so and it should be encouraged. This position has great opportunity to build strong student relationships.

• The ISS supervisor must understand that the purpose of ISS is not to punish; it is to teach.

• The ISS supervisor is able to create an environment that is emotionally safe and unconditionally accepting to the students assigned to ISS.

WHAT HAPPENS ALL DAY IN ISS?— When students are assigned to ISS for disciplinary reasons, one of the first priorities is to check in on them to see how they are doing. Taking time to process what happened to place them in ISS is essential. Getting them to not only express the logistics of the event, but also what emotions they were feeling and what level of overwhelm they were experiencing is important to helping them learn self-awareness skills.

Helping these students to process how they could do things differently the next time and what positive coping mechanisms they could do in the future is vital to helping them change their patterns. Doing this within the context of a safe, non-judgmental, and accepting relationship is the key. Once the student is reconnected in relationship, has had a chance to vent his feelings and be heard, and is regulated back down to a top-down control, that is when the cognitive work can begin to help the student with his learning and improving his coping skills.

The ISS is certainly a place where students can do their school-work so they don't fall further behind academically but it is just as important to use the time in ISS for the "teaching moments." On the following page are important tools and skills to teach these students:

• Regulation strategies
• Social language skills

- Social interaction skills
- Emotional intelligence
- Emotional expression
- Communication skills

Students will learn these skills and tools better if they are taught through interactive ways such as:

- Role playing
- Behavioral rehearsals
- Relationship building

A PLACE TO REGULATE—The ISS is not only for helping students after they've demonstrated negative behaviors, it can also be used in a proactive way to prevent negative acting-out behaviors. If the school does not have a calm room, the ISS room can be used instead.

- If Billy was up all night due to high family stress or domestic violence, have him use the ISS room to get some down-time or needed sleep. It's a place for students to get rejuvenated and then return to their classes.

- ISS should be available to students asking for a personal timeout. This is a positive strategy for students to learn how to self-regulate their stress and know when they are getting close to that fight-flight-freeze mode.

ADMINISTRATION'S ROLE—The administration's role is to stay attuned to the operating procedures of the ISS and the implementation of these procedures. The administrator needs to make sure everybody involved with the ISS (ISS supervisor, teachers, and students) is fulfilling his/her role as this is critical to the smooth and effective operation of the ISS. Here are a few pointers to keep in mind:

- When first implementing the ISS, explain the new format for using in-school suspensions and the philosophy behind it. Let staff know how you are going to structure ISS and the ISS room. Clearly explain all the operating procedures.

- ISS will be assigned by the office as a consequence to a school infraction but it can also be used by teachers when

"It's critical that children spend time before they arrive in school in a warm, attractive and inclusive environment, where they can learn through play, master social skills, and prepare for formal schooling."

– Michael Gove

> *"The greatest gift that you can give to others is the gift of unconditional love and acceptance."*
>
> *– Brian Tracy*

students need a regulatory break to calm down.

- Most students do not want ISS. They would rather have an out-of-school suspension (OSS), which to them is a vacation from school.

- Because students prefer OSS, sometimes they will threaten to disrupt ISS if you do not give them OSS. You can respond by saying, "'Wow, you are going to take a suspension day and then come back and still do your ISS day? If I were you, I'd rather get it done as quickly as I can, but it's your choice. I would hate to have to suspend you and then have you still come back for ISS." (Stay consistent on this...most will not disrupt, but you have to be prepared for those who do.)

- When talking to students who are dealing with issues that could cause a disruption at school, value their input and lay down the expectations in a caring but firm manner. If you have a school resource officer (SRO), have him or her sit in on the conversation. A SRO creates a strong presence.

- The administration can assist the ISS program by making it clear to staff that if they have one of their students in ISS, they are responsible for getting the work to the student.

- Bring in students you know are having issues and sit them down to seek the cause of their tension. Let them know that you really care about them and you are being proactive. Explain to them how they can use the ISS room when they need a break.

TEACHERS' ACCESS TO ISS—There needs to be active communication between teachers and ISS. Traditionally, once a student was removed from the classroom, that was it. The teacher continued teaching the rest of the class and the office took care of the discipline. There was a complete division between these two places. Such an approach is too fragmented and disrupts the consistency of relationships. Instead, the teacher and the ISS need to be interactively involved.

- Teachers need to be able to access ISS so they can send a student for a break or send a student who is having a rough day and needs some quiet time.

- Teachers can send a student to ISS if he/she is disrupting the learning environment and the student isn't responding well to the teacher's regulatory efforts.

- Teachers should always notify the office if they are aware of any student assigned to ISS if they feel the student needs additional support or follow up.

- Teachers can use the ISS as a way to help students take responsibility for their next steps by giving students the option of going to ISS or staying in class if they feel they can engage.

> **Always notify the ISS supervisor when and why you are sending a student to ISS. If student does not make it to ISS, the supervisor will alert the office.**

Teachers should NEVER use ISS in a punitive way. It is to be used with the intention of helping the student and for the student's own wellbeing. Students learn that it is not a punitive consequence but rather an option for getting regulated so they don't become more disruptive. Teachers can use the ISS in a way that says, "I'm here to help you, not punish you." For example, a teacher might say to the student, "I am really trying to work with you and give you an option (the ISS room) so you can get your stress down and be successful in class."

Sometimes students will continue to make it an issue because they are programmed to see being removed from the classroom as a punishment. They can get defensive, irritated, and defiant but remember that these are learned responses from years of being in punitive environments. Teachers can simply let students know that their brains are not in a good place for learning and reassure them that once they feel they are ready to come back to the class and engage, they are welcome. If the student remains defiant then a referral to the office will be necessary.

FLEXIBILITY VS. RIGIDITY—Traditionally, once a punishment is given, it sticks. From a behavioral perspective, it has been seen that rules are rules and they must be adhered to, no matter the circumstances.

Complete rigidity doesn't help the trauma-impacted student. Yet on the flip side being too relaxed and not holding strong boundaries can also be detrimental to helping these students. However, there is a middle ground that is important to consider when working with this population. The typical trauma-impacted student has a very low sense of self; they see themselves as the "bad" student and they reject themselves as most

"I am a man of fixed and unbending principles, the first of which is to be flexible at all times."
— *Everett Dirksen*

adults have done in their lives. They feel completely powerless and typically feel that nothing they do—good, bad, or otherwise—can make a difference.

For these reasons, you may consider working with these students when they have been given ISS. When they are able to show effort and make changes, these changes need to be acknowledged. When a student's pattern is to give up and stop trying to be good it takes a tremendous amount of self-control, self-motivation, and courage to take steps in the right direction. We have to begin to see that the changes that look small to us, are huge changes to them and they need to be recognized. Here are two examples of how you can do this:

"We think sometimes that poverty is only being hungry, naked and homeless. The poverty of being unwanted, unloved and uncared for is the greatest poverty."

– Mother Teresa

- If a student has been assigned a few days to ISS, check in with the student to keep building your relationship with him/her. If you find that the student is working hard with a great attitude, pull the student into the hallway and let the student know how much you appreciate them taking responsibility and working hard. You might even consider telling them to go back to the regular schedule due to their accomplishments, giving them the sense that they do have control over how their lives unfold when they make the effort.

- Unless there is a safety issue, you might consider allowing students in ISS to attend one of their classes, such as science, if the teacher requests their presence. This gesture shows students that you don't want them to fall behind and it shows your trust that they will come back to ISS when the class is over.

Most students will recognize when you are honoring their attitude and work ethic. If you cut them loose a day, they won't let you down.

If this is challenging your thinking, consider that traditionally, we didn't have strong foundational relationships with our students. When the relationship isn't there, it's easy for a student to say, "Ha! Look what I just got away with, sucker!"

With this model however, students have a desire to respect you because they have a relationship with you. True control comes from the power of influence, not through fear. These students are learning what it means to be in reciprocal relationships that are being built through trust, acceptance, and a sense of belonging. Underneath all the trauma is little boy or little girl that simply wants to be loved, seen, and feel special. You have the power to reach this inner child in each of your students through the power of your relationship and with the ability to be flexible.

ADDITIONAL NOTES ABOUT ISS—Besides the information above, the following are additional tips to running an effective ISS:

- If patterns begin to surface and students are taking advantage of using ISS as a means to get out of a specific class, then this issue needs to be addressed in the office.

- The ISS supervisor should alert the office of any personal issue with the student in which they may need counseling or additional support and follow-up.

- If a student is disrupting ISS and everything has been done to help the student regulate back down, the student should be referred to the office.

- If students stay home purposefully to miss their ISS assignment, the day is considered unexcused and they are still required to do their time in ISS.

"Accountability Prevails"

LINCOLN HIGH SCHOOL
BY JIM SPORLEDER

Soon after implementing our ISS, I had a student in my office who was part of our "Frequent Flyer Club." He was always in trouble and was used to having out-of-school suspensions. He didn't like the new change and did everything to try to get me to suspend him instead of having to go to ISS. The conversation unfolded like this:

Me: "Billy, you're going to have to go to ISS for the afternoon."

Billy: "Nope, I'm not going to do it. I'll take the suspension."

Me: "I'm not suspending you."

Billy: "Well, you're going to have to because I'm not doing ISS."

Me: "Yes, you have to go down and do ISS."

Billy: "Sporleder, if you send me to ISS, I guarantee I will do everything I have to do to get kicked out of ISS and then you will have to suspend me."

Me: *(Throwing my arms up in the air dramatically but playfully)* "Oh my...Oh, you're killing me here. I'm asking you to do half a day and you want me to suspend you. Now you're telling me you are going to force me to suspend you? Why would you do that because when you come back the next day, you'll be in ISS?"

Billy: "No I won't. If you suspend me, I don't have to do ISS."

Me: "I'm not suspending you."

I literally had students begging me to give them an out-of-school suspension instead of giving them ISS. To them, ISS was boring compared to being home or out on the street on their own.

A trauma-informed model holds students more accountable than any traditional model. In a trauma-informed model, you keep the discipline in school as much as possible. This makes the student accountable for coming back to school the next day. He comes to school and his work is brought to him so he isn't falling behind. This is why it is critical to match the right person for the ISS room. The supervisor has to be a nurturing and caring adult to make it work.

CHAPTER NINE

Students of Concern

The importance of creating an entire school atmosphere of addressing the emotional and relationship needs of all your students cannot be emphasized enough. This is true whether students are Andys or Billys. It is important to note that even if Andy hasn't been impacted by trauma, he has emotional and relationship needs. This model still applies to him yet not typically at such an intense level.

Focusing on the general emotional, social, economic, psychological, and academic needs of your students will be enough for the majority of your students. However there will be some students who will need additional support. These are the students who traditionally have been seen as the "bad" students or the "disruptive" students...those students who were simply expected to change, follow the rules, and be like Andy.

As we implement the understanding of what trauma does to our Billys, it becomes easy to see that this idea of a Billy stepping-up and being an Andy on his own is almost impossible. What happens is that Billy becomes more of a Billy, with the eventual outcome of either failing, dropping out of school, or entering our juvenile justice system. The reality is that children do not grow out of trauma, they grow into it.

In an effort to prevent this outcome, a "Students of Concern" (SOC) list needs to be created to be able to clearly identify and support these students. Our Billys do have the ability to become Andys...it just takes relationship vigilance with the proper interventions.

"Few people are mind readers. Let them know they matter."
– Dr. Chris Peterson

Identifying Students—Some students will be added to this list as a response to an infraction that has already occurred but ideally, students will be added to the list in a proactive manner. The earlier you can identify students at-risk, the better. Traditionally, disciplinary interventions have only been "after the fact" which only makes it harder to move the student back into a state of balance and academic success. This model works to identify students before the behavioral collapse happens so early interventions can be implemented.

TRADITIONAL INTERVENTION

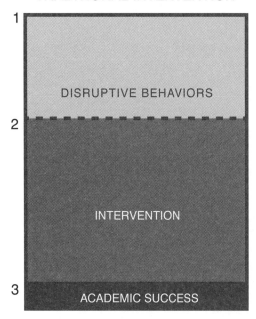

TRAUMA-INFORMED INTERVENTION

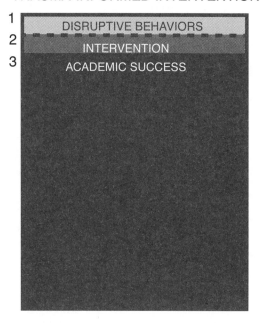

Proactive measures along with identifying disruptive behaviors early, lead to easier interventions and more academic success.

SOC Form—Any staff member concerned about a student's well-being should take the time to identify this student to the SOC Team Leader. The procedure for this is to fill out a SOC form (see the Appendix for an example) and give it to the SOC Team Leader. On the following page is a list of reasons a student would be identified as a student of concern:

- Academic Struggles

- Alcohol Use

- Anger Issues

- Anxiety (Nervous, Tense, or Tearful)

- Attendance

- Current Abuse

- Dating Issues

- Death of a Family Member

- Death of a Friend (Student)

- Death of a Friend (Non-student)

- Depression

- Destruction of Property

- Drug Use

- Excessive Absences from Class

- Family Issues

- Financial Concerns

- Friendship Issues

- Gender Identity Issue

- General Behavioral Issues

- Homelessness

- Identity Issue

- Illness

- Injury

- Isolating and Disconnecting from Peers

- Lack of Participation

- Low Frustration Tolerance

- Mental Health Issues

- Notable change in Appearance

- Overreaction to Circumstances

- Past Abuse

- Poor Decision-Making

- Poor Hygiene

- Self-Injurious Behaviors

- Student/Teacher Relationship Issues

- Substance Abuse

- Threats to Others - Bullying

- Too Many Tardies

"Fire can warm or consume, water can quench or drown, wind can caress or cut. And so it is with human relationships: we can both create and destroy, nurture and terrorize, traumatize and heal each other."

– Dr. Bruce Perry

- Witness to an Incident

- Other

Please Note: Immediate concerns that cross the line of safety such as suicidal thoughts or ideation should be dealt with immediately. Either the school has a designated person fully qualified to deal with such a crisis with a well defined protocol or it needs to be reported immediately to a community mental health agency or 911. It is extremely important to recognize that there will be some cases that are out of the realm of the school, and these cases need to be passed on to those with more experience and qualifications.

If a teacher notices any of the above concerns regarding his/her student, simply completing a SOC form and handing it to the team leader isn't the right approach. The first course of action is for the teacher to tap into the power of the teacher/student relationship. The teacher needs to first make every effort to support and help the student. The teacher/student relationship is very powerful and it needs to be the number one priority for every teacher, especially for the Billys that are of concern. The teacher needs to have exhausted all his/her resources with this student and then, if change hasn't been possible the teacher needs to elevate her concern to the next level (filling out the SOC form and giving it to the SOC Team Leader).

It should be mandatory that forms must be turned in prior to the SOC meeting so that time is not wasted.

"Traumatic stress impacts a developing child's brain. Clarity of thought, sequential thinking, and speed of processing can be severely hindered. Or as one child put it, 'I feel like I have cobwebs in my brain!'" — Heather T. Forbes, LCSW

SOC ACTION STEPS

Teacher identifies student and takes extra steps on her own to work with the student.

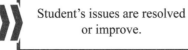

Student's issues are resolved or improve.

No further action by the teacher besides staying closely connected with the student.

Student's issues do not improve or they worsen.

Teacher completes a SOC Form and gives the form to the SOC Team Leader.

SOC Team Leader adds student to the SOC Document.

SOC Team Leader opens the conversation about the student at the next SOC meeting.

Issue is determined to be a teacher issue.

Teacher is given support and the issue is addressed without the SOC Team.

The Team agrees the student needs to be added to the SOC Document.

An Action Plan is developed and added to the SOC Document.

Staff member is assigned to the SOC to oversee and ensure the Action Plan is implemented.

SOC Team—The SOC team should be made up of the entire school or a least one representative of every grade, discipline, and academic focus, depending on the size of the school. A SOC Team Leader needs to be identified and appointed. This individual will be responsible for processing all SOC forms to ensure each student reported is brought to the attention of the entire SOC team, and that an action plan is created and implemented.

SOC Meetings—SOC meetings should be held at least once a month but for maximum effectiveness, meeting at least twice a month has proven to be better. Depending on your enrollment, SOC meetings can be organized into grade level teams or in any way that you feel will serve your school most effectively.

At first you will see staff identifying students based off of their behavior, but eventually you will see staff shift and start to identify students based off of other factors: attendance, mental health concerns, substance abuse concerns, or information about a crisis a student or family is going through.

Be sure to continually reinforce the entire list of reasons for identifying students listed in this chapter to expand the thinking of your teachers and school personnel. Most operate from a behavioral platform and are not attuned to looking at students from a holistic perspective.

"You might not be able to reach 100% of your students, but you can love each one of them 100%."

– Jim Sporleder

The recommendation would be to have the SOC Leader and another staff member run the SOC meeting. The SOC Leader needs to structure and guide the meeting, keeping it focused and on track. It's not set up to be a complaining session; rather, it is a process to address student concerns. While the SOC Leader guides the discussion, the other staff member is documenting the information being shared on a laptop. An action plan is developed and assigned before addressing the next student concern.

An emotionally safe and open environment needs to be created at each SOC meeting and it is the SOC Leader's responsibility to set the tone for each meeting. The following are steps that need to be taken when a discussion is opened regarding a student that has been identified on a SOC Form:

1. The SOC Leader identifies the student and identifies the issues listed on the SOC Form, "Billy is struggling in Teacher A's class. He has been consistently tardy, isn't completing his work, and is very disrespectful to Teacher A."

2. Teacher A shares more about his/her concerns and gives more understanding and details regarding the identified issues.

3. The other teachers share their observations and experiences of Billy. Patterns and triggers are identified regarding Billy's behaviors.

4. A determination is made as to whether this is an issue with the student overall or if it is a clash between only Teacher A and Billy. If it is the latter, the student is not added as a SOC but individual support is given to the teacher and the clash is worked through without the team. If it is the former, the student is added as a SOC and the meeting continues its focus on this student.

5. An action plan is developed and documented on the SOC document.

6. A staff member is assigned to overseeing Billy and implementing the action plan. This staff member documents the results of the intervention and the date in which it took place on the SOC document. It is very important that this staff member completes the action in a timely manner as it shows the staff that their concern and input is taken seriously and that a plan is put into place.

SOC Document—The SOC Document is a chronological list of each SOC with his/her action plan. The SOC document can be uploaded to Google Docs so it is accessible for viewing by all the staff. However, only a few have administrative access to modify the document (such as the SOC Leader, Principal, and Behavioral Interventionist).

The SOC document runs continuously through the school year. If there is a second SOC on the same student, then the documentation and action plan will reflect the new intervention that is going to be put into place and the results. Some students will only appear for a short time on the document, other students will have a greater focus and more office interventions.

The SOC document covers the following:

- Name of the student
- Grade level
- Staff member reporting the concern
- Issue(s) of concern

"Relationships matter: the currency for systemic change was trust, and trust comes through forming healthy working relationships. People, not programs, change people."
– Dr. Bruce Perry

- Action plan

- Person assigned to implement the action plan

- Outcome

- Date completed

It is important to make sure outcomes are documented on the SOC spreadsheet so that staff is aware that action was taken on their concern. This will keep staff motivated and confident their voices are heard and that their concerns are being taken seriously.

When a student successfully turns a situation around, it is documented but is not removed. If the student is still coming up at the SOC meetings, then a stronger action plan needs to be put together until there is change in the student's behavior, attendance, or classroom participation.

"You cannot force a child's healing process, only support it."
– Heather T. Forbes, LCSW

Interventions—Each situation with a SOC will vary, however here is a list of suggested interventions:

- Meet with the family at the school in a non-threatening and supportive atmosphere.

- Make home visits—bring Billy to school if he has not been attending.

- Communicate with probation officers using a collaborative model, not a punitive one.

- Find help for homeless students (food, clothing, shelter).

- Consider a placement in a woman's shelter due to potential abuse or domestic violence (there may be an age restriction of 18 years old to have access to services).

- Find assistance for families in crisis.

- Collaborate with community partners to refer family issues outside of your service capabilities.

- Access available health care for students and find referrals for mental health, medical, and other services.

- Partner with law enforcement and juvenile justice center on safety issues.

"Let It Out"

ELEMENTARY SCHOOL
BY HEATHER T. FORBES, LCSW

I was consulting with a school and was in a fourth grade class observing. While I was there, I noticed a young lady who was having difficulty managing herself in the classroom. She was constantly doing things to get the teacher's attention and she kept looking back at me to see if I would notice her.

A couple of hours after I had left the class, her teacher called for help with this Billy. She had become frustrated with the teacher, ran out of the class, and was hanging around in the hallway near the classroom. They asked me to intervene so I went down and found Billy crying and standing near the door.

I approached her slowly and said, "Hey, Billy. It looks like you're pretty upset with your teacher." She didn't say anything but kept crying.

I didn't ask her anything about what made her upset. I simply said, "It's okay to cry...just let it out, Sweetheart." And boy did she let it out at that moment! The tears were flowing, the nose was draining, and she sat down and had the biggest cry. I sat down next to her and encouraged her to keep letting it out.

After a few minutes, she stood up and went and stood on the other side of the hallway near a locker. I slowly got up and went over to her, keeping a little bit of a distance because she didn't even know me and we had no relationship. At this point, she started kicking the locker, not too hard but enough that I knew she wanted to say something. When kids start banging things and making noises, it is usually a sign that they want to be heard.

The conversation unfolded like this:

> Me: "What did your teacher do that made you so angry?"
>
> Billy: "She hates me! She likes everyone in the class but me!"
>
> Me: "That's not very fair, is it?"
>
> Billy: "No! She's just like my grandmother. She hates me, too!"
>
> Me: "Oh...dear. What's going on at home?"
>
> Billy: "She took my brothers and sisters to Florida without me this week!"
>
> Me: "I'm so sorry. That must really hurt."

We talked a bit more and I simply validated her reality and her feelings. I didn't try to fix the situation for her and I didn't try to convince her that her teacher really did like her. She was fairly calm at this point so I said, "Are you ready to go back to class?" She nodded her head yes. I also offered to go in with her, "Do you want me to go in with you?" She said, "No, it's okay" and she headed back into class.

For the moment, this crisis was resolved fairly easily. However, the underlying issues of this Billy were not addressed. Identifying this Billy as a SOC would be ideal to get ongoing interventions and supports in place. Having an action plan in place would help prevent further downward spirals and would be the perfect way to help to get her back on track.

CHAPTER TEN

Creating a Relationship-Based Culture

A trauma-informed school isn't solely about changing how students are disciplined or how to de-escalate students. It goes much deeper than this. It's about how both the staff and the teachers view each other as human beings—how everyone is viewed as an important part of the entire synergistic whole.

A trauma-informed school is a place where more importance is placed on relationship than on the curriculum. While this may seem counter-cultural and a devastating perspective when it comes to funding policies that are based on academic scores, the irony is that this is exactly what it takes to excel academically—and even more so when it comes to educating the Billys of the classroom.

Step back and look at this thought purely from a cultural perspective (let go of test scores, funding, and graduation rates for just a moment). What would make you happier, working at a school that is fraught with negativity, unhappiness, and struggles or at a school that is positive, uplifting, and balanced? The obvious answer is the latter.

The science of happiness is a growing field and it is showing that those that are happier are better able to self-regulate, and they have lower levels of the stress hormone cortisol. Both of these are foundational principles to creating a successful trauma-informed school. Additionally, environments that support the happiness and well-being of individuals are intrinsically emotionally safe and calming.

The ultimate goal of any school should be to create a place worth being for its own sake, academics aside. It should be a place where students would want to be even if they weren't mandated to be there. Especially

"You may say I'm a dreamer, but I'm not the only one. I hope someday you'll join us. And the world will live as one."
— *John Lennon*

for our Billys, such an environment is what is critical for reaching and teaching them.

Great school cultures are built, they don't just come into being by accident. It takes demonstrating genuine interest and concern for each student of the school to foster a culture of family and connection.

The relationships between administrators and staff set the tone for the entire school. Truly we must see that administrators' relationships with their staff impact the staffs' relationships with their students. If you're going to create an atmosphere of relationship and caring, the principal and the rest of the administrative staff need to take the lead for the entire school.

Traditionally, schools have had more of an "us against them" culture. Switching that around, a trauma-informed school must have an "us with them" culture.

Strategies—There are several strategies that need to be implemented to make this happen. If you use the strategies listed below, it will help guide your success in establishing a relationship-based and trauma-informed climate. The following are based off of lessons learned through the implementation of a trauma-informed culture at Lincoln High School in Walla Walla, Washington:

HIGH VISIBILITY AND SUPERVISION

- It is essential to have high visibility to create opportunities for developing caring adult relationships with your students and supervising with close proximity to influence a safe school environment. Wander the building looking for students who might be isolated and make sure they are recognized and valued for being at school.

- Be present during transition times and when students are gathered together and socially interacting. Research shows that the safest schools have staff highly visible before school, during passing time, at lunch, and after school.

- Be vigilant for students who appear angry or upset. Be cognizant about following up with them and checking in with them. Remind them they don't need to be alone in their struggles and if they need any help, you will be there for them or can find the appropriate resources for them.

"The quality of your life is the quality of your relationships."
— *Tony Robbins*

- If you observe a student that is escalating, invite them to come with you in a supportive, non-punitive way. Try saying something like this, "You're not in trouble. I'm just here to support you and help you. Let's go take a break." The stronger your relationship is with this Billy, the more likely he will be able to step away from whatever it is that is igniting him in that moment.

- If a student expresses that they are really having a bad day, share your concern for their stress load and ask if they need a place where they can calm down.

- Don't put students back into the classroom unless you are confident that they are calm enough not to go back and create a disruption.

- It is very important that you have support staff available during the lunch hour to mingle with the students and to monitor student-to-student interactions. If you sense that there is tension between two students or you see gang tension, intervene right away or place a staff member in very close proximity to the students to discourage anything from happening. If something does begin to ignite, this staff member will be able to step in immediately. Relationships are hard for all of us, especially our Billys so constant contact and constant vigilance is going to be critical.

- When you become aware of student tension, be consistently proactive. The old adage, "An ounce of prevention is worth a pound of cure" holds true in this context. As information is passed on to you, step into the tension instead of stepping away to see what happens. As discussed in earlier chapters, Billys don't know how to problem solve. Their relationship negotiating skills and ability to see other people's perspectives has been compromised due to trauma. Bring the students to the office and ask them, "What is happening?" Let them know that you are aware that there is conflict and get their side of the story...let them have a voice. Guide them and teach them how to resolve conflicts appropriately. These are golden healing moments you don't want to miss.

- Always take the opportunity to share that you really care about them, and that you do not want them to make a choice that would disrupt the school environment.

- Reinforce the rules and hold the boundaries but do it in a caring and compassionate way (see the next chapter for more on this). The school is a public setting and students

"I find the best way to love someone is to not change them, but instead, help them reveal the greatest version of themselves."

— Dr. Steve Maraboli

"Much like addictive drugs, power uses ready-made reward circuitries in the brain, producing extreme pleasure."

– Nayef Al-Rodhan

should be held accountable if they bring disorder into the school and threaten the safety of others. Rules of safety are an absolute, but we must also recognize that Billy doesn't have strong internal controls or a working moral compass. He needs the adults around him to create an external environment that can handle him and guide him. Billy needs to be lovingly taught that schools are public institutions and the law prohibits people from disrupting public entities. Remember that so many of our Billys come from home environments that don't have any boundaries. Billy is simply working from a dysfunctional blueprint and thus, needs guidance to understand the rules of reality.

• If you sense a potential fight, make sure you have your school resource officer in the room with you when you speak to the student about potential consequences if there is any physical aggression or verbal disruptions that threaten the safety of any student, including them.

• When you pull students aside who are gang affiliated or have a history with disruptive classroom behavior, this is a great time to let them know how much you appreciate their respect and keeping their word of "leaving their colors on the curb" (leaving the violence outside). It allows you to keep to your commitment of treating them respectfully and at the same time you are reinforcing the subtle message that the conversation would be different if you had to deal with an incident.

GREET STUDENTS IN THE MORNING

• Greet students in the morning by name. By doing this each morning, you are building relationship and setting the tone for the day.

• As you have students being greeted as they come to school, you are visible to any outsiders wanting to come on campus and it gives parents a sense of safety to see that there are adults supervising.

HAVE A PRESENCE DURING PASSING TIME

"Using a person's name is crucial, especially when meeting those we don't see very often. Respect and acceptance stem from simple acts as remembering a person's name and using it whenever appropriate."

– Dale Carnegie

• When possible, staff should stand at their classroom doors during passing time, greeting students and engaging with them as they enter the classroom. Giving students instructions as they enter the classroom helps to guide them into a successful and positive transition. Getting students engaged right away can prevent down-time which only gives Billy more opportunity to be dysregulated and create more dysregulation amongst his peers.

- Staff proximity and visibility is a proactive way to keep out-of-class disruptions and conflicts from happening but more importantly, it gives staff more face time to build and reinforce relationships.

- Engaging with students during passing time also allows staff to pick up on any body language or potential conflicts that should be reported to the office for follow-up. Coach staff on becoming the observers and how to be attuned to the students. It simply takes noticing students from a loving standpoint, without judgment or criticism. Watch. Just watch. And you will see how much information is being expressed in the non-verbal communication of your students.

CONNECT WITH STUDENTS IN THE CAFETERIA

- Have a person located in the cafeteria greeting students as they come in for breakfast. This is an excellent time to circulate and build positive relationships as well as identify any students that who may need a follow-up. It's a good way to set the tone for the day.

- At lunch, station your supervision so that you have staff circulating, interacting, and talking to students. Some staff will have a tendency to simply stand and only watch students. This is ineffective as it sends the "us against them" culture instead of the "us with them" culture. Be sure to coach your staff on how important it is for them to connect and interact with the students. This includes both the outgoing students as well as the quiet introverted students.

- Make certain those talking with students are looking to see if there are any hot-spots brewing so that you can follow-up with early intervention. This social environment is an excellent opportunity to catch conflicts from further developing within the school setting.

BE THE LAST CONTACT AFTER THE DISMISSAL BELL

- It is so important to be highly visible in front of the school as students are being dismissed. Be the last contact they

"Good Morning! Good Afternoon! Good Night! These are not just mere greetings. They are powerful blessings, setting the best vibration for the day. Hence, whether it is morning, after-noon or night, make sure that you say your greeting right!"
— *Franco Santoro*

have as they leave the school campus so they are returning back home as regulated as possible.

- Ask students how their day went, thank them for working hard, and tell them to have a great afternoon and to be safe.

- Let your students know that you look forward to seeing them tomorrow or on Monday.

Examples of Connecting—The following are phrases to help you when connecting with your students and to help build the culture of relationship in your school. It is important, however, to say these phrases not from an intellectual or cognitive place but from a heart-centered and nurturing place within you. It's not so much the words that are important as are your intention, affect, and sincerity.

- "Good morning, Billy! It's great to see you today."

- "Billy, you've made my day by coming to my class!"

- "Great to see you, Billy. How was your weekend?"

- "See you tomorrow, Billy. Have a great day!"

- "Hey, Billy. How are your classes going?"

- "Billy, I have to tell you...I am so appreciative of your positive attitude. You've really changed things around. I'm so proud of you!"

- "Billy, I know I've said this before but I want to make sure you always know that if you need anything—anything at all—come to the office and let me know."

- "Billy, just checking in with you to see how it's going. Anything I can help you with?"

- *For new students, let them know you are glad they are at your school:* "Billy, so glad you're here with us at our school. Let me know what I can do to help you feel welcomed!"

"Relationships are the agents of change and the most powerful therapy is human love."

— *Dr. Bruce Perry*

Relationships are an art. Not all students are going to respond initially and that's okay. It is your message that is setting the climate. Unconditional acceptance is one of the foundational principles of a relationship-based platform. This means you offer connection without expecting anything in return. The less you require a student to respond back positively, the less stress you create in the interaction thereby creating a connection that is much safer and much more inviting. The irony is that the less you expect students to respond, the more they will.

If you find it annoying, disrespectful, or rude if they don't respond back to you in a respectful and appreciative manner, try to remember that such interpretations were developed from a traditional, fear-based, and control-based platform. Part of you is probably saying, "But it's just good manners to respond back respectfully." And the answer is yes, yes it is.

However, forcing a positive response only adds more stress and you'll stay in the same negative cycle with the student. Give the student space and some time to come back around to you. Stay consistent. Stay the course. Stay focused on the process. Love will win. It always does.

"My Heart Grew Bigger"

LINCOLN HIGH SCHOOL
BY JIM SPORLEDER

Billy transferred into our school and she was an extremely angry person. In the mornings, we would greet her and she would just bark back at us:

Me: "Good morning, Billy."

Billy: "What's so good about it?!"

One morning, her comment back to my greeting was, "You better tell Andy to keep her mouth shut or she's going to have my fist in it!"

I let her go on through to class but once school got started, I brought her into my office. I had the SRO (Tom) just sitting there to create a presence and I said,

> *"Billy, at Lincoln, we really care about our kids. The comment you made this morning concerns me because it referenced you punching somebody. If that were to happen, I'd feel horrible because then Tom would have to put on his policeman's hat and he'd have to take you to JJC (Juvenile Justice Center). I just wanted to connect with you and hope that you don't actually follow through with that threat."*

Then, Tom made his comment, reinforcing what I was saying yet doing so in a calm relationship based manner.

Nothing further happened that day and we continued to greet her every morning, giving her reassurance that she was welcomed at this school and that she was a special part of the entire student body. Her defenses started lessening; her attitude started softening. She then starting coming into my office to talk to me on her own.

About this same time at Lincoln, word of what we were doing started to spread and I was receiving books from people offering more resources to support us. One day as our relationship was growing, Billy came in to my office to chat and apparently during the course of the conversation, she asked if she could read one of the books.

A week or so later, she came back to my office and here's how the conversation unfolded:

Billy: "Hey, do you have time to talk to me today?"

Me: "Of course, what's up?

Billy: "My heart's grown bigger."

Me: "Well how does your heart grow bigger?"

Billy: "Do you remember that book you gave me?"

Me: "No...(laughing)."

Billy: "Sporleder, it was right on your desk and I asked you if I could have it. You said yes."

Me: "I'm glad you have it...I just don't remember which one it was."

Bllly: "Well, it's helped me a lot!"

Me: "Tell me about it."

Billy: "Well, I learned that in order to go forward in my life. I have to be able to forgive my past. I called my dad over the weekend and I forgave him for all the horrible things he did to me."

Me: "Where did you ever get the strength to do that?"

Billy: "Because I want to be able to move forward."

Sometimes you have to start slowly, little bit by little bit, offering students kindness, relationship, and acceptance. They may not respond positively right away, but when you stay consistent and hold strong, amazing changes are possible.

CHAPTER ELEVEN

Accountability Comes Through Relationship

With all the previous chapters describing how it is necessary to be nurturing, connected, and accepting with Billy, it could easily lead one to the belief that a trauma-informed model is all about letting students do what they want, without consequences or any type of accountability. However, the exact opposite is true.

In fact, a trauma-informed school could never function successfully without strong boundaries and without holding students accountable! These are precisely what make this model so successful. However, it takes a delicate combination of being soft, kind, and loving while also being strong, unwavering, and bold.

Mister Rogers vs. General Patton—Billy needs you to be both empathetic to his struggles yet at the same time strong enough to handle him. In essence, he needs you to be a hybrid between Mister Rogers and General Patton.

"Ironically, real 'power' and 'control' come from your influence with a child, not through your dominance over a child."

— Heather T. Forbes, LCSW

© The Fred Rogers Company, used with permission

© Bettmann/CORBIS, used with permission

"Never tell people how to do things. Tell them what to do and they will surprise you with their ingenuity."

– Gen. George S. Patton

If you're 100% Mister Rogers, giving Billy all understanding with no boundaries, Billy won't respect you and he will walk all over you. Additionally, Billy won't feel safe with you. Billy doesn't know where the boundaries and limits are because he has grown up in a family that is enmeshed and without structure. Billy needs you to hold these limits so he can understand when he does cross the line. Simply telling him the rules and describing the limits won't work. He has to experience crossing the line in order to comprehend it.

Yet, enforcing the rules and boundaries with an iron fist, devoid of all empathy will feel to Billy like you are simply trying to control him. A child who has experienced life at the level of survival will never allow such a dynamic. Hence, being 100% General Patton will only create more conflict, disobedience, and resistance.

Students impacted by trauma are chaotic on the inside so they need the people closest to them to be strong, clear, consistent, yet nurturing, accepting, and empathetic. Standing strong with them, not against them, shows them you care enough about them and they "matter." It sends a powerful message that they are important enough for you to spend the time and energy to hold the line for them.

When students keep pushing the limit, they are typically described in a negative way: "He just keeps testing me!" The answer is yes. Billy doesn't know the limit, so he needs to keep testing and testing to see where the limit is. It is important to hold this line consistently in order for Billy to learn exactly where "enough is enough" (General Patton) but in a loving and kind way (Mister Rogers).

Billy is the type of student that seems to take advantage of the smallest little leeway you give to him: "You give him an inch and he takes a mile!" Again, taking the Rogers/Patton approach will be necessary to help Billy learn how to stay within the boundaries.

"Love isn't a state of perfect caring. It is an active noun like struggle. To love someone is to strive to accept that person exactly the way he or she is, right here and now."

– Fred Rogers

Compare the two examples on the next page between a full-blown Patton approach and that of a Rogers/Patton approach.

	PATTON	PATTON / ROGERS
PRINCIPAL	"Billy! You know the rule. No phones. Give me that phone now. It's no longer yours. It's mine."	"Hey, Billy. You're texting and the rule is no phones. Everything okay?"
BILLY	"Hell no! It's my phone. I paid for it."	"Yeah, I'm just talkin' to my peeps."
PRINCIPAL	"The rule is NO PHONES! Give it to me now otherwise you will be serving time in detention or worse."	"I'm glad you have friends, Billy. That's good. But, the rule I have to enforce is no phones and I know that's really hard to stick to all day long at school, isn't it."
BILLY	"No! You're not taking my phone. EVER!"	"Dude, it's totally impossible!"
PRINCIPAL	"Yes, I am. I'm in charge. You don't have a choice in this. Either you give me the phone now or I'm calling the resource officer right now."	I know. How about this…how about you give me your phone to hold on to for the rest of the day. I'll keep it safe and I'll give it back to you when the last bell rings? That way, you don't get into trouble and you get your phone back so you can continue connecting with your peeps at the end of the school day?"
BILLY	"F***!" *And he hands the phone to the principal.*	"Seriously?"
PRINCIPAL	"You just earned yourself a day of suspension for that language. Keep it up and you'll get more days."	"Yes, I know. It's hard. You've got a passcode lock on it, so no one can read your private information."
BILLY	"What the f***?! I just gave you my G** D*** phone like you told me to!"	"Okay, Sporleder, but you promise I get it back at the end of the day, right?" And he hands the phone to the principal.
PRINCIPAL	"Okay, now you have two days suspension."	"Absolutely. I appreciate you trusting me and letting me support you."

In the first approach (Patton), it was a "me against you" unfolding throughout the entire dialogue. The principal got the phone but the relationship became even more strained due to this interaction, and the student's anger escalated to the point his language was out-of-control. By the end, the student is suspended for two days to be left to his own devices in the community, likely without any supervision.

In the second approach (Rogers/Patton), it was a "me with you" unfolding throughout the entire dialogue. The "consequence" regarding the phone was the same—the principal confiscated the phone—but there was enough empathy and understanding expressed that the relationship actually improved. Additionally, the student will remain in school under close supervision with people who care about him and can continue to help him learn to regulate and take responsibility for his actions.

It may take a bit more time and energy using the Rogers/Patton approach in the short-term, but the long-term benefits will far out-weigh the time and energy you invest in these interactions.

"Say what you mean and mean what you say."
– General George S. Patton

Discipline, Accountability, and Punishment—When first implementing a trauma-informed model, one of the hardest aspects to wrap your brain around is the idea of not punishing students for negative behaviors. Wouldn't your school be complete chaos without consequences?

The answer is yes. Without boundaries or consequences, it would definitely be a "free-for-all." However, the shift comes in the delivery of the consequences and the understanding of how we should guide our students to take corrective action. The definition of discipline is to teach, not to punish.

Punishment drives disconnection. It strengthens the "me against you" platform. While discipline, when delivered within the context of a relationship in a loving manner, builds connection. Discipline strengthens the "me with you."

Discipline also holds students accountable. Holding students accountable is extremely important as it sets the bar for students who do not have the family support they need. Students who don't have expectations ingrained into them will float. There is nothing to strive for and nothing to push up against. They become easily lost in school and in the world.

For example, here is a comment from a high school senior who was not held accountable for his attendance:

"I graduate Wednesday. I'm still kind of mind f***ed by the whole thing. I've missed 90% of high school. I only go like once a month so its just kind of weird that I'm actually going to be done with it, considering I feel like I never really even went to high school. And now its already time for college."

Not holding students accountable is confusing to them. It creates a world of chaos and instability for them...they don't know where the limits and boundaries are. Not having structure, expectations, or boundaries creates a world that doesn't make sense to them. They're not grounded and they have no clear direction.

More importantly, it gives them the message that they aren't worthy. In this example, one of the deepest burdens we bear as an educational system is that we haven't made this student feel important. When we step in and hold students accountable, it gives them the message that they are worthy and their lack of attendance at school is a loss to the school. This message was never given to this student and now he is entering the "real world," with not only a lack of education but a lack of worthiness.

Stress and Behavior— As discussed in Part I, when students are regulated, they can think clearly and they have a greater ability to understand the feelings of others. Thus, when students are regulated, it is easier for them to follow the rules, act appropriately, and be courteous to others. In the following graphic, the dashed line represents the rules and the boundaries. When regulated, notice how the student is within the established limits.

"In times of stress, the best thing we can do for each other is to listen with our ears and our hearts and to be assured that our questions are just as important as our answers."

– Fred Rogers

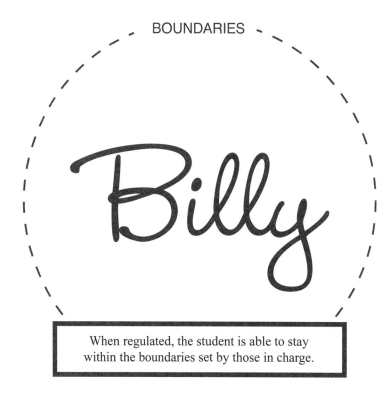

BOUNDARIES

Billy

When regulated, the student is able to stay
within the boundaries set by those in charge.

However, in the next graphic (again, the dashed line represents the
rules and boundaries), the student is outside of the established limits.
The reason for this is because he is stressed, dysregulated, and/or
overwhelmed.

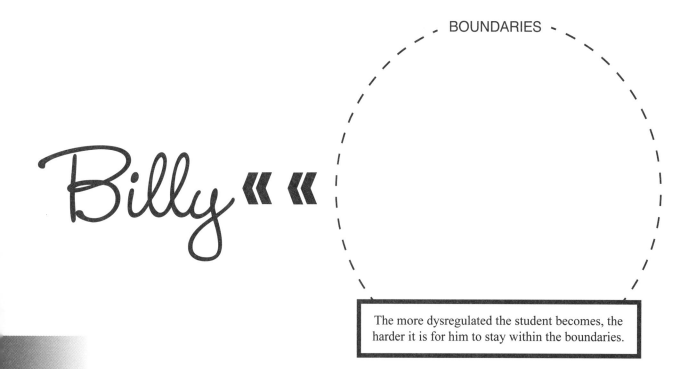

BOUNDARIES

Billy «
«

The more dysregulated the student becomes, the
harder it is for him to stay within the boundaries.

If you give the student in the second graphic a punishment in an attempt to move him back into the boundary, he will only become more stressed out and with a typical Billy, his negative behaviors will likely increase.

The solution is to first connect with the student. Ignore the behavior for the time being. Suppress your desire to teach a life lesson in the moment, for now. Instead, check-in with Billy about what is going on. Relate to Billy from the heart-level instead at the intellectual or cognitive level for now.

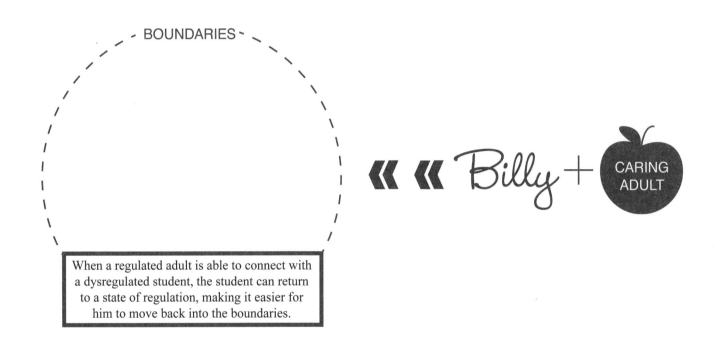

When a regulated adult is able to connect with a dysregulated student, the student can return to a state of regulation, making it easier for him to move back into the boundaries.

When you teach students about stress and the impact it has on their behaviors, you can get students to start owning their stress levels. Teach them what it means to use a scale from 1 to 10 regarding how stressed out they are. Then, when you are interacting with a student who is clearly stressed out, a dialogue can unfold similar to this:

> Principal: "One to ten, where's your stress, Billy?"
>
> Billy: "Nine!"
>
> Principal: "It's unfair to ask you to function when you're that stressed out, Billy. We have to get your stress level down. What do you need? You can go to the ISS room for a bit and calm down or you can take a break with me and

talk about what's driving all this stress. Which one works for you?"

In this scenario, you're acknowledging that it's hard to function at a high level of stress but you're not "letting the student off the hook," either. You are giving him two direct non-negotiable choices. The message is being sent that you will not tolerate his behavior, yet you're doing it in a regulation-focused and relationship-based manner. Additionally, the "consequence" of being removed from the classroom is also happening.

Notice that in this dialogue the principal said, "WE have to get your stress level down," instead of "YOU have to get your stress level down." This, again, reinforces the "me with you" platform. It also alleviates any blame and it sends the message, "You're important enough to me that I'm here to help you."

If Billy were to choose the second option, this would be an excellent opportunity to find out what is really behind the negative behavior and the inflated stress level. This would also give you a time to teach the student how to identify his triggers and how to start becoming aware of how the triggers show up first at the body level. By asking, "Where in your body do you feel the stress?", you are helping the student learn how to own the stress before it owns the student. You'd be giving Billy tools to be responsible for his own stress level in the future on his own.

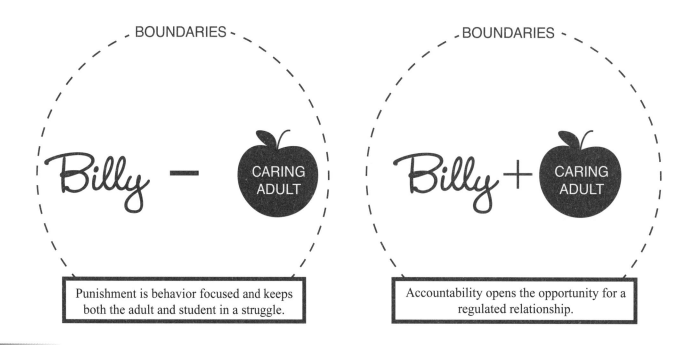

BOUNDARIES

BOUNDARIES

Billy — CARING ADULT

Billy + CARING ADULT

Punishment is behavior focused and keeps both the adult and student in a struggle.

Accountability opens the opportunity for a regulated relationship.

Punishment may be able to get students back into the boundaries and it may change their behaviors temporarily, but the relationship suffers. For long-term success at a school with children impacted by trauma, this will never be the solution. Instead, staying relationship and regulatory focused allows us to teach students responsibility and it keeps them accountable. But more importantly, it builds their ability to trust people again and to develop a stronger sense of self that will equip them to achieve academically now and in the future.

What to Say—Most of us did not grow up with people in our lives who implemented the Rogers/Patton approach. We grew up with pure Patton responses such as, "I'll give you something to cry about!" or the like. Below is a list of phrases you can begin to practice to train yourself to be a combination of Mister Rogers and General Patton to your students. As you do this more often, you'll be able to come up with the balance yourself, using your own words:

- "I can see that you seem really upset. What do you need from me to help get back to calm?"

- "I'm really trying to work with you, but you seem so upset I am not helping. What do you need from me right now?"

- "You're too important to me to not help you learn right from wrong."

- "This is too big to try to handle by yourself. Let me support you."

- "I know you're not going to like me having to enforce this rule because its no fun to have other people in charge of you, is it?"

- "Billy, you seem really agitated. What's really going on?"

- "We need to be able to work together, Billy. What do you need from me so that you will be okay and I can teach?"

- "You're right, it isn't fair. You're so right about that! But I'm here with you to help you work through all the rules of the school, even when they don't seem fair."

- "What else isn't fair?"

- "What other rules don't you like about this school?"

- "How about I come back and check on you in about 10 minutes? I want to make sure you're okay."

- "You seem upset. How can I help? Do you want to put your

"I'm convinced that when we help our children find healthy ways of dealing with their feelings—ways that don't hurt them or anyone else—we're helping to make our world a safer, better place."
– Fred Rogers

head down on your desk until you feel better, or do you want to go to ISS for a break?"

- "I don't know where the 'F-you' came from; I care a lot about you, please go to the office and I'll follow up on how you are doing later."

- "Billy, I did my best to try and solve the problem with you. Can we work this out the simple way or do you need to go to the office to work through this issue?"

- "This assignment seems like it might be hard for you, may I sit with you and help you get through the parts that seem difficult?"

- "Billy, I care too much about you to ignore that you are refusing to do your work. I'd be happy to sit with you and help you if that's what you need, or I will help you during lunch. What will work best for you right now?"

Create some of your own responses from interactions you've had in the past:

- _____
_____

- _____
_____

"Part of the problem with the word disabilities is that it immediately suggests an inability to see or hear or walk or do other things that many of us take for granted. But what of people who can't feel? Or talk about their feelings? Or manage their feelings in constructive ways? What of people who aren't able to form close and strong relationships? And people who cannot find fulfillment in their lives, or those who have lost hope, who live in disappointment and bitterness and find in life no joy, no love? These, it seems to me, are the real disabilities."

— *Fred Rogers*

"From Exploding to Advocating"

LINCOLN HIGH SCHOOL
BY JIM SPORLEDER

Before this student even arrived at Lincoln High School, I got involved with Billy (a middle schooler at the time) because he had made some dangerous and inappropriate comments about a girl. This girl's parents came in to report the incident and it was determined that the threats were serious enough to be investigated. The consequence of this young man's actions ended with him being expelled from his middle school. The entire ordeal was a huge challenge and for a variety of reasons, the entire process of carrying out the expulsion was horrible. It truly was one of the ugliest incidents I'd been a part of in my history as a principal.

A couple of years later, Billy showed up at Lincoln as a freshmen. We knew we were facing a challenge and the teachers were saying, "If somebody is going to come to this school with a gun, it will be this kid."

So I kept saying, "Build the relationship; build the relationship." The first year was indeed a challenge and Billy kept making inappropriate comments to other students in class; he was creating quite a stir. The teachers, however, made a turn and started to accept him and connect with him. We started loving him and it worked.

As a freshman, he was in my office for something he was doing in class but then he started to tear up. Billy asked me, "Why were you so mean to me when I was in middle school?" I said, "I didn't make those decisions but I'm so sorry it was such a horrible experience," and we were able to talk through it.

This young man grew so much over the next several years. By the time Billy was a senior, he was a completely different student. I was doing several tours of our school when Billy was a senior and Billy was the one who would stop and welcome these guests to our school. He would be walking down the hall, see us, and say, "I'd like to welcome all of you to Lincoln High School." Instead of the Walmart greeter, Billy became the Lincoln High School greeter!

Billy took such pride in our school. He became the student that was giving other students the message that they had to represent the school in a positive way. When we had visitors who wanted to know more about the school from the student's perspective, I would have Billy come and talk with the visitors. I'd leave him on his own with them. They were absolutely blown away by how insightful Billy was and how much he absolutely loved his school. In the end, the student who was feared to be the kid who would bring a gun to school became our school's greatest advocate.

As I got to know and understand Billy, I found out more about his family life and how difficult it was for him. His parents had divorced during his time at Lincoln High School and he lived with his dad, with whom he had a loving relationship. However, his relationship with his mother was a different story. As a senior, Billy came into my office one day and asked if he could talk to me. He shared with me that his mother said to him, "I wish I had aborted you...you should not even be alive!" I was able to be there in his pain with him. From my heart I said to him, "Billy, if we didn't have you here at this school, we would have lost this opportunity to know one of the most incredible kids ever." He came over and just buried his face in my chest. I held him and he wept—just wept. Then he pulled his head up and looked me straight in the eyes and asked, "Why would a mother ever tell her son that she wished he wasn't alive and that she wished she'd killed him by aborting him?"

After graduation, Billy continued on at the community college and today works with his father in their family business.

CHAPTER TWELVE

Effective Use of Your School Resource Officer

Having a School Resource Officer (SRO) at your school can be a wonderful addition to implementing a trauma-informed school, as long as the SRO is trained in this trauma-informed model and understands the importance of using the Rogers/Patton approach. A SRO who is 100% Patton will likely undermine all your best efforts in making this model effective.

Safety is one of the key purposes of having a SRO on campus but as the previous chapters have pointed out, one of the most effective strategies to creating safety is relationship. The SRO will be the most "Patton" person on campus, but it is also very important to make sure this individual works to foster better relationships between law enforcement and the students. The goal is to stop the school-to-prison pipeline, not strengthen it. Thus, the SRO needs to be a part of the staff training and needs to make a personal commitment to support the path in which the school has chosen to take.

Because of the safety factor that the SRO represents, the SRO has the capacity to play one of the most vital roles in the success of your trauma-informed school. If possible, the SRO should have his/her office in the main office of the school. Use the SRO as a proactive team member of your office team.

SRO Strategies—Below is a list of ways you can use your SRO in a proactive and interactive way to create both safety and relationship and thus, strengthen your trauma-informed school. Many of these will take some conscious work and energy upfront, but such efforts are the best way to ensure safety in your school.

SELECTION OF THE SRO—If your school is in the process of hiring a SRO or replacing your current SRO, the principal should meet with the chief of police or supervising sergeant to clearly identify the job responsibilities and expectations of the SRO. The principal and a trusted staff member, well educated in the trauma-informed model should be on the interview team. The principal should have input on interview questions, most of which should focus on whether or not the SRO has the mindset and willingness to work from a trauma-informed platform.

COMMITMENT TO THE MODEL AND TO THE TEAM

"The greatest power is often simple patience."
– E. Joseph Cossman

- The SRO has to first agree to the paradigm shift and agree to be an active part of the team. If not, a meeting with his/her supervisor may be needed to set the expectations.

- The SRO should be a part of all staff development on the trauma-informed model.

- The SRO should feel like an inclusive part of the team and be willing to cooperate as a team member, rather than an isolative individual at the school.

- The SRO needs to understand the magnitude of the impact that the title of "School Resource Officer," has on the students when he/she offers this caring adult relationship.

- The SRO's duties are to build positive student, staff, and community relationships, and to make sure the school is safe. It is critical that the principal clarifies this boundary with staff as to the intended use of the SRO. The SRO should never be put in a position to do school discipline. The SRO's responsibility is to keep the school safe from a legal perspective. It is important that staff understand that the SRO is not to be involved in any school discipline. It actually puts the officer and school in a liable situation, and it will undermine his role with the students. Here are two typical and common examples:

    1. A staff member asks the SRO to arrest a student for telling her to "F-off." This would not be a legal issue for the SRO but certainly a disciplinary issue for the school.

    2. A student walks off campus and ignores a staff member's request to stay on campus so the staff member reports the incident to the SRO with the expectation that the SRO will arrest the student. Again, this is not a legal issue but rather a disciplinary issue.

3. In the beginning, the SRO should meet with the principal for mentoring and regular "check-ins" to discuss scenarios and answer questions as the SRO works to embrace the trauma-informed model. The trauma-informed model is very different from your typical police training, so regular meetings at least every two weeks are going to be critical to ensure a successful application of this model. If the learning curve is poor and the SRO simply isn't "getting it," then the SRO needs to be removed and replaced.

INTERACTIONS WITH STUDENTS

- The SRO needs to be part of the team that is highly visible in the morning, greeting students as they come to school. This sends the message, "We are glad you're here but we are serious about safety."

- The SRO needs to be consistent and visible at lunch and be back with the team wishing the students a good afternoon as they leave campus at dismissal.

- The SRO should take on an advocate role. When students experience this, they will respond to him in a positive manner.

- The SRO needs to see that talking to students and getting to know them, is time well spent. These simple, yet powerful interactions are the most effective proactive strategy. This should be embraced by the SRO because a trust will develop in which the students will seek out the SRO's help if they are having problems outside of school or if there is something brewing in school that they're concerned about.

- The SRO should be willing to extend his/her monitoring outside of the school campus. If there is concern of an off campus conflict, the SRO should be out in his/her police vehicle traveling the streets close to school checking to see if there is any intervention needed for proactive prevention.

- It is very important for the SRO to walk the building or campus while students are in class. The SRO should vary his/her route and the timing of the route so students can't predict his/her routine.

"Leadership is about making others better as a result of your presence and making sure that impact lasts in your absence."
— Sheryl Sandberg

ESTABLISHING STRONG LIMITS

- Students should see the SRO in a positive light but they also should clearly understand that if they break the law, there

"Power is of two kinds. One is obtained by the fear of punishment and the other by acts of love. Power based on love is a thousand times more effective and permanent than the one derived from fear of punishment."

– Mahatma Gandhi

will be legal and school consequences. They need to see the Patton side of the SRO but not in a fear-based way. Rather, they need to see the SRO's Patton side so they know if their internal systems become too chaotic, there will be someone who can handle them. A tremendous amount of safety is created when students know the limits will be enforced. It makes life predictable and creates certainty.

- If there is an issue that you feel might turn into an altercation, have the SRO sit in on the conversation when you bring in the students with whom you have the concern. Here are a couple of examples of how the SRO can set the tone and reinforce the safety limit:

  - "I really care about you kids, but if you disrupt the school environment or have physical contact, you put me in a position in which I may have to arrest you and take you to JJC. I'm here to make sure everyone is safe, always."

  - "I am part of this team and it is my responsibility to keep a safe environment for all students. It would be very disappointing if you choose to make me put on my law enforcement hat. I would rather see us problem solve and take care of the problem so nobody goes to juvy."

- There will be times when all you have to do is have the SRO present at the time you are speaking to the student(s). The SRO's presence is a strong silent message without words.

- Over time, the students see the SRO as part of the school staff. If available, the SRO should be at the table whenever there is a conversation with any student over a concern of an incident happening at school. The SRO's presence alone sends the message that your school is serious about enforcing the rules. Yet, the conversation remains focused on intervention and prevention with empathy.

- Consistency is very important. What happens to one student happens to the others. Students need to see the fairness of the consequences upon all their peers.

- If an angry parent comes to the office highly escalated and/or threatening, the SRO needs to make himself visible while the staff person works to let them know their voice is important. Connect with the parent but set the boundary, "I want to help you but I can't help you if you're yelling at me." When the SRO is present in a situation such as this, what happens most frequently is the parent will cease the verbal threats and aggressive behavior.

• If there is rumor of potential gang violence from gang members who are not students, it's helpful to have the SRO's police car parked where there is greatest visibility. The same would be true if drug dealing was rumored to be happening in close proximity to the school.

When Billy Breaks the Law. A student who has committed a serious infraction, such as an assault or gang fight, needs to be arrested to send the message that if a student brings his colors into school, then it is going to be taken very seriously. However, if a student has to be arrested, he should always be treated with respect and his dignity is of top priority.

The typical procedure in schools is to handcuff the student so other students can witness this punishment. The belief is that this will deter other students and reinforce that the school won't tolerate extreme behavior. However, this approach shames the student being arrested and further isolates the student from his peers and his school family. It reinforces the "me against you" platform that is divisive and fear-based, and it only serves to add more trauma to the student's life.

There will be isolated exceptions to this rule when safety is at stake. If a student becomes threatening due to a mental health issue such as a psychotic break or due to a drug-induced state, physical intervention at that moment will be necessary. A student in a psychotic state or high on meth has no ability to connect and be rational and can actually be very dangerous. Empathy and relationship-focused conversations are ineffective and physical intervention is truly necessary when it gets to this point.

However, it cannot be emphasized enough by the authors that these are the exception and when you implement a trauma-informed platform successfully, the times of needed physical restraints will be the rarity at your school. For most students, staying close to them and staying relationship-focused will be enough.

If Billy commits a minor first offense, yet is cooperative, tells the truth, and takes responsibility for his actions, the SRO should consider writing up the charge but not arresting Billy. Billy should be told that his honesty and cooperation is being honored by charging him with only a ticket instead of arresting and handcuffing him. Despite this, however, Billy should still be held accountable for the charge and school consequence.

"Never forget that the most powerful force on earth is love."
— *Nelson Rockefeller*

In the cases where Billy has to be arrested, consider the following options:

OPTION ONE:

- When Billy's attitude and level of cooperation are reasonable and he owns up to his actions, the administrator should talk to him before he is going to be arrested.

- To reduce the fear, the administrator should tell Billy what is going to happen. The administrator should start off by telling Billy that he wants to be respectful and that he doesn't want any surprises. Billy may not like what the administrator has to say, but Billy will know the administrator cares.

- Because he has been cooperative, the SRO should let Billy know that he still deserves respect and that he wants to protect his dignity. To do this, the SRO should wait for the other students to be in class before he makes the arrest.

- If Billy remains cooperative, the SRO should allow Billy to walk to the police car before he is handcuffed. Students really appreciate it when they are shown this kind of respect. They are more often remorseful for their actions and apologize.

OPTION TWO:

- Sometimes students will have a serious enough offence that the SRO has no other choice than to arrest Billy in that moment. To minimize the drama of such an incident, the use of handcuffs needs to be done in the office, if possible.

- Billy should be handcuffed and walked out to the police car when the other students are in class. He needs to be treated with respect despite his behavior.

"Knowledge will give you power, but character respect."

— Bruce Lee

When a student is being arrested, the SRO is taking on the Patton role so this leaves the administrator the opportunity to be in the Mister Rogers role. Stay in relationship with Billy and avoid lecturing Billy. This is not the time to teach the life lesson. The reality of the situation is doing the teaching for you at this moment.

Be empathetic—It is fair to gently express to Billy how disappointed you are that he made the choices he did, but reassure him you'll be here when he returns with open arms. Give him the hope of a new beginning once he returns. "Billy, we can start over when you're back. We will be here to help you succeed, no matter what."

Whenever possible, if an office person can go to the detention center and process with the student while being locked up, it really sends the message to the student that you really do care. It demonstrates unconditional love and acceptance.

Even if the student is "guilty" of the charge, it doesn't lessen the amount of fear that comes with this type of consequence. Developmentally, many of our 17- and 18-year-old Billys are really just little boys or girls on the inside. Billy may look and act tough on the outside, but inside his/her grown-up body is a scared little boy or girl. Be there in the fear and you will earn the respect of this student for a lifetime.

"Be there in the fear and you will earn the respect of this student for a lifetime."

Unconditional Acceptance

LINCOLN HIGH SCHOOL

JIM SPORLEDER

A gang fight broke out between two students but fortunately, the two students (Billy-1 and Billy-2) were separated quickly. While Billy-1 was in the office, he simply wouldn't calm down, despite all our best efforts. The SRO deemed the situation serious enough to call in back-up. When Billy-1 saw the other officers he went ballistic. He stood up and hit his fist through the wall, shoved the two officers out of the way, and headed towards where Billy-2 was being de-escalated.

The officers yelled for him to stop but Billy-1 was on a mission to get to Billy-2 and yelled, "F-off!" The officers tased Billy-1 and he face-planted screaming. The officers cuffed him and took him in.

Within an hour, we were with Billy-1 to show unconditional love and support for him. At this point, even locked up, he was calmer and expressed to us how bad he felt for doing what he did. We stayed and processed with him and told him we loved him. Before we left, we hugged him. Billy-1 was touched so deeply, tears were rolling down his face.

Today, Billy-1 is out of the gang. When he sees me out in the community and we run into each other, Billy-1 bear hugs me from the bottom of his heart each time.

CHAPTER THIRTEEN

Tracking Dysregulation Through Behavior

This trauma-informed model does not focus on behavior initially; it recognizes that a student's behavior is dependent on the student's state of regulation. If you work to help a student regulate through relationship, then the result will be positive behaviors. Behavior simply gives insight into a student's level of regulation.

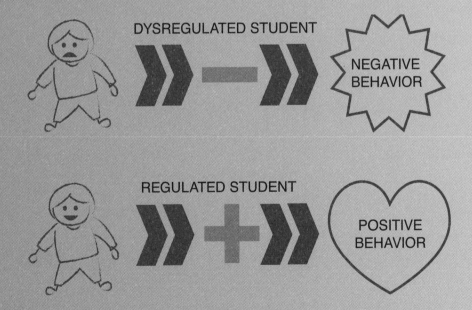

From the illustration below, we see that students on the dysregulation spectrum are either hyper-aroused or hypo-aroused. Hyper-aroused students will show outwardly signs of being dysregulated with behaviors such as talking back, arguing, aggression, impulsivity, and risk-taking behaviors. On the other hand, students who are hypo-aroused will go inward with their behaviors. These are the silent students who may not appear to be "behavioral problems" but are dysregulated to the extent that they shut-down, withdraw from peers, become defiant, look "lazy," are tardy, and seem to be continually forgetful.

	REGULATION	
	• Responsive	
	• Engaged	
	• Focused	
	• Calm	

DYSREGULATION	DYSREGULATION
HYPER—arousal	HYPO—arousal
• Impulsive	• Tardy
•Aggressive	• Absent
• Argumentative	• Defiant
• Anxious before tests	• Forgetful
• Resistant to directives	• Avoids tasks
• Risk-taking behaviors	• Withdraws from peers
• Cannot adhere to rules	• Disassociates—shuts down
• Unable to focus or sit still	• Numbs out—"I don't care."
• Yelling	• Depressed
• Threatening	• Crying

This trauma-informed model is always aiming to help students get back into a state of regulation because that is where students are able to have positive behaviors and will be able to be responsive, engaged, focused, and calm.

Traditionally, we have tracked behavior simply for behavior's sake. In this model however, we will also track behavior but the distinct difference is that we are tracking behavior in order to understand the state of regulation of our students.

Thus, tracking behavior will also include factors that help to identify why the student is dysregulated. Tracking behavior will require more than a simple check mark or a point system with levels. It goes much deeper than a simple numbers game.

This trauma-informed behavioral tracking will be a much more wholistic approach to understanding the student's emotional, social, economic, and academic well-being—all factors that contribute to the student's level of regulation, and thus, the student's behaviors.

"Too often we forget that discipline really means to teach, not to punish. A disciple is a student, not a recipient of behavioural consequences."

– Daniel J. Siegel

Factors to Track—The following is a list of the factors you will want to track for each student that is referred to your office:

1. Name
2. Grade
3. Teacher Writing the Referral
4. Ethnicity
5. Free/Reduced Lunch
6. Special Program (Special Ed, ELL, or Behavior Program)
7. Self-Identified Level of Regulation (Scale of 1 to 10)
   - Pre-test – Beginning of the office visit
   - Post-test - End of the office visit
8. Self-Identified Level of Social Connection
9. Self-Identified Level of Feeling Physically Safe at School
10. Infraction
11. Consequence
12. Parent or Guardian Contact Documentation
13. Arrest, Citation, or Neither (for secondary schools)

Most of the factors listed above are self-explanatory. The following are more in-depth explanations for the few that warrant further discussion:

7. SELF-IDENTIFIED LEVEL OF REGULATION (PRE- AND POST-)– When Billy first comes into the office after being referred by his teacher, ask him, "On a scale from 1 to 10 (10 being the highest), how stressed-out are you?" If Billy is giving a high number, you'll know that it will take time to help him get settled and calm. Your conversation at this point needs to be relationship and regulatory focused only. Do NOT get into logic, rational thought, expectations, or explanations as to the rules and policies. Remember from the earlier chapters how Billy is in his emotional brain when he is highly dysregulated; rational and logical thought cannot be processed easily while in this state.

At this point, simply connect with Billy. Listen to his side of the story (even if it is skewed and out-of-reality). Don't try to convince him of anything. Just let Billy have a voice and ask exploratory questions ("What happened next?", "How'd that make you feel at that point?", "Who else was bothering you?", etc.). This will allow Billy to vent and feel like he is important and worthy.

DYSREGULATED

Listen
Connect
Empathize
Accept
Tolerate
Validate
Love

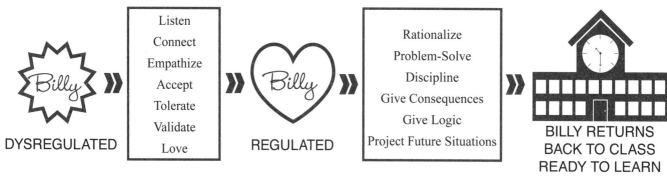

REGULATED

Rationalize
Problem-Solve
Discipline
Give Consequences
Give Logic
Project Future Situations

BILLY RETURNS
BACK TO CLASS
READY TO LEARN

Once you notice Billy starting to calm down and becoming more regulated, then you have a student who is functioning from the part of the brain that can comprehend sequential thinking, logic, and cause-and-effect thinking. This is the time to problem-solve and talk about what consequences will be part of the disciplinary action you have to take. This is also the time to help Billy think about how he will handle similar situations in the future.

Getting Billy to the point where he is regulated enough to talk to you can be within moments or sometimes it may take awhile longer. You can't force a student to regulate. Billy may need more time to be "pissed-off" and angry. In times like this, allow Billy to sit in a calm environment until he is ready to talk. He may need to go to the Calm Room or ISS and take a time-out. This time-out, however, is not a punitive measure; it is simply giving Billy the time and space to settle his nervous system. Once he is calm, then it is time to talk, teach, and problem solve.

When this conversation is over but before Billy is ready to go back to class, ask him, "Where are you now on a scale from 1 to 10 in your stress level?" This will be the post-test to be recorded on the *Behavior Tracker*.

> *"The ability to read social cues and respond appropriately during times of conflict is compromised by traumatic experiences."*
> — *Heather T. Forbes, LCSW*

8. SELF-IDENTIFIED LEVEL OF SOCIAL CONNECTION—As human beings, we are biologically designed to be in community; we are social creatures. When we don't feel connected to people and to the world, we easily slip into a state of dysregulation. This is especially true for Billy.

One of the main goals of this trauma-informed approach is to make certain every student in the school feels connected and socially accepted. Thus, when Billy is sent to the office, it will be important to check in with him to see how he perceives himself in his school "family." Ask Billy, "On a scale of 1 to 10 (10 being the best), how well do you fit into this school and feel as if you belong here?" Record this score on the *Behavior Tracker*.

If Billy gives a low score, this is not the time to try to convince him he is misperceiving his importance in the school. Simply recognize his reality, empathize with him, and make a note to have him added to the SOC list to create an action plan to get him better connected.

9. SELF-IDENTIFIED LEVEL OF FEELING PHYSICALLY SAFE AT SCHOOL—Many of our Billys live in crime ridden neighborhoods and rarely, if ever, feel safe at home. For these students (and of course for all our students), it is especially important that they feel safe at school. When a student feels unsafe at school, it peaks his arousal system and increases his stress level. Many times this factor alone can result in negative acting out behaviors for students.

The *Behavior Tracker* needs to identify the level of physical safety students who are acting out feel at school. This may be an indicator that more efforts need to be in place to create a stronger feeling of safety and security within your school. When Billy walks into the office because of a referral, ask Billy, "On a scale of 1 to 10 (10 being the safest) how safe do you physically feel at school?"

It's Not Just About the Student—Being a relationship-based model, it is important to look at the dynamic between both the student and the teacher. This is a dyad between two people who are interacting with one another.

Thus, the *Behavior Tracker* also tracks the referring teacher. This is important to identify because you may begin to notice the Pareto Principle (also known as the 80/20 Rule) playing out whereby 20% of the teachers are making 80% of the referrals.

When staff members become reactive and are unable to maintain their own level of regulation, you will see a direct correlation in the number of students being referred to the office by them. This is the perfect opportunity to use this model with these staff members. When questioning yourself about a particular teacher, ask yourself, "What is driving this teacher's reactivity?" Instead of simply dealing with the behavior, you have to dig deeper to understand the resistance, fear, overwhelm, or stress that is a part of this teacher's world.

If you see a specific staff member writing excessive discipline referrals, it's a good conversation starter to bring him/her in and ask how you can be of support. In a nonthreatening manner, you can share with the staff member that you have noticed they have written excessive office referrals when compared with the building average. Perhaps you start the conversation by saying (in a calm, non-judgmental tone), "While tracking our school discipline, I have noticed that you are at the excessive end of writing discipline referrals compared to your peers. Most of your referrals are centered around _____ (insert *identifying issue*). Share with me some strategies that you have tried that aren't working for you."

Work to understand the staff member. Validate how challenging the

"The 'soulution' to working with challenging children is to live at the soul level and stay in your heart. There you will find the answers."
— Heather T. Forbes, LCSW

Billys are in their classroom. Recognize how difficult it is to switch an entire paradigm of thinking into a trauma-informed model. Remind the staff member that they are an important part of the team and that the team is less effective without them. Be Mister Rogers to get to the root of the issue. Always stay in a, "How can I support you?" stance.

Most staff members will respond positively to your supportive conversations with them. However, there will be a few who, no matter how hard you try, will not be able to make the shift into this new trauma-informed way of thinking. Eventually, you may need to hold a strong Patton boundary. While you typically don't have the ability to fire them or transfer them, you may consider using some of the following statements and questions to come to a mutual agreement that they need to find another place of employment:

- "Not everyone can teach in this environment."
- "It takes a different way of thinking to teach here and this way of thinking may not resonate with you."
- "Do you feel like this school is a good fit for you?"
- "Perhaps there is another school that you would find more fulfilling and more aligned with your core beliefs?"

Do not get into a control battle with resistant teachers; it is unproductive. This type of interaction only fuels them (which is probably why they aren't doing well in a trauma-informed school that is all about de-escalating and relating to students). Give it back to them to make the decision. You can also try to work with the personnel director and be a creative problem solver with this issue.

If they end up staying on staff, you will still be able to make this shift to a trauma-informed school work. All and all, when you have the majority of your staff on board with this model, it won't take away from the momentum. The success of a trauma-informed school requires a collective approach, and you'll still have this from most of your staff members.

"When you are creating change and asking others to cross the bridge in their approach, don't get inpatient and burn the bridge you want others to cross."

– Jim Sporleder

Using the Behavior Tracker — Here are a few key points to keep in mind when using the *Behavior Tracker*:

- The *Behavior Tracker* is designed to track your office

discipline referrals per each school year.

- Have one person do the implementing of data so the infractions are consistently recorded.

- In order to track your discipline referrals and progress, it is imperative that you develop a system that keeps you current with implementing the data into the spreadsheet.

- The *Behavior Tracker* allows you to sort the information you are seeking and it keeps a running record of the monthly data for discipline. In the future, you will be able to make comparisons as you start your second year of implementation. This is a great tool to let you know how you are doing in comparison with the first year of implementation.

  - You will have data to show the improvements you are seeing with your students.

  - This data gives you feedback to share with staff if you are seeing a specific issue reoccurring that needs greater supervision or awareness.

  - It gives you a way to commend your staff on the work they are doing with keeping students in class or using strategies that allow students to de-escalate and keep them in school.

  - The *Behavior Tracker* is a tool that is in alignment with state-mandated reports on suspensions, emergency expulsions, expulsions, and weapons report.

- The *Behavior Tracker* can be adjusted to your individual or district needs, giving you flexibility.

The following is an example of the *Behavior Tracker*. It is also available for quick reference in the Appendix.

BEHAVIOR TRACKER FORM

NAME	GRADE	TEACHER	RACE	F/R	SLR PRE	SLR POST	SLSC	SLFS	INFRACTION	CONSEQUENCE	P/G CONTACT	ARREST OR CITATION

F/R: *Free or reduced lunch* | *SLR PRE: Self-identified Level of Regulation when student enters office* | *SLSC: Self-identified Level of social connection*
SLR POST: Self-identified Level of Regulation at end of office visit | *SLFS: Self-identified Level of physical safety at school* | *P/G: parent/guardian*
SLSC: Self-identified Level of Regulation at end of office visit

"I Hate This F---ing School"

LINCOLN HIGH SCHOOL
BY JIM SPORLEDER

I think it is critical to seek support around students who are frequent flyers to the office for classroom disruptions or blowing up at their teachers. One specific student, Billy, was at his traditional high school and was blowing out of classes, skipping school, and being suspended for swearing at teachers. He was then referred to Lincoln.

When Billy first arrived at Lincoln, he told me it was the best school he had ever attended but within a few weeks, his behavior patterns started to surface and he was once again being referred to the office. His level of disruption was over the top and the teachers were unable to keep him in class.

Billy was being referred by a variety of teachers who were typically very good at calming students down, but with Billy, it wasn't working. When he was referred to the office, it was a challenge to help him to regulate his anger and defiance:

> Me: "Billy, what is going on that is causing the blow-ups? You keep getting referred to the office."

> Billy: "I hate this f---ing school! I want to go back to my old school."

> Me: "Billy, it would be difficult for us to lose you as a student but if you really want to go back to your other school, we can make that happen. However, they won't allow you to go back unless you are passing all of your classes. They have to see that your behavior has improved."

> Billy: "Anything to get out of this f---ing school! I hate the teachers here; all they want to do is get me into trouble."

> Me: "Billy, we are a family. We love all of our students and we love you."

> Billy: "That's bull----! You guys don't care about me! Why am I being sent to the office everyday?"

> Me: "Billy, I respect your opinion. However, your feelings are your feeling and our feelings are that we love you. You ask a very good question, why do you think that the teachers are referring you to the office?"

> Billy: "I told you! They hate me and they want to blame me for everything just to get me into trouble."

Billy became a top priority at the Student of Concern meetings and we were implementing an "action plan" to provide interventions for him. We had a couple of staff members who volunteered to make it a top priority to build a caring adult relationship with him. We also set up a parent conference as part of his action plan.

At the parent conference, Billy was very disrespectful to his mother and started blaming her for his problems at school. I could see that his mom was trying to be firm and hold Billy accountable but she really struggled with follow-through. The consequences that she had put into place at home were not being used to define the boundaries and Billy just blew them off. My conversation with Billy and his mom went something like this:

> Me: "We want to work with Billy and create a positive school environment for him to be successful and feel valued. However, Billy is struggling to stay within the boundaries that we have set for him at Lincoln. Billy is having some major battles and disruptions with some of his teachers. I need feedback from you and Billy. I don't think it is fair to Billy or his teachers to have daily blowups and to have Billy

failing his classes. Billy, you need to tell me which classes you think that you can be successful in and which classes we need to drop since we are in a no win situation. However, I want you to know that whatever classes we drop, it will put you further behind in your credits towards graduation."

Billy: "I don't want to drop any of my classes; I just want the teachers to leave me alone and quit getting me into trouble for nothing."

Me: "Billy, you need to let me know which classes you want me to drop until the end of the quarter and if you want to add the classes back into your schedule, I'm willing to do so if your class disruptions have improved. Or if you are doing well, I will honor your request to go back to the high school you transferred from."

Billy: "I told you that I don't want to drop any of my classes! You're taking the teacher's side and wanting to kick me out of school."

Me: "Billy, if I had my wish, I would want you to stay with your regular schedule and not having you blowup at your teachers each day. I'm willing to go with your choice but if you are referred for disrupting the classroom and not requesting a break so you can stay regulated, I will begin to shorten your day."

Billy: "I want to stay with my full schedule."

Me: "Great, just make sure if you feel your trigger is about to go off, you come see me so that I can provide a quiet place for you to calm down."

We did not have to shorten Billy's schedule and he slowly began to use the timeout opportunity to regulate himself back down instead of blowing up at his teachers. When the quarter ended, I called Billy in to see if he still wanted me to honor his request to go back to the high school from which he transferred. His answer was, "I don't ever want to go back to the f----ing school!"

CHAPTER FOURTEEN

Implementing the Trauma-Informed Model

Switching to a trauma-informed model is an exciting journey and once you start moving forward, you will never look back. This is the model that changes lives of trauma to lives of hope and resilience, one relationship at a time. Before the first day of school, it will take doing ground work to prepare for a successful first year. This includes making sure your staff is trained, welcoming new students to school, and establishing the paradigm shift that will set the tone for the entire year.

Staff Development—A minimum of one full day of staff development needs to be created to teach staff about trauma and how the school will be shifting to a trauma-informed approach. To facilitate this staff development, create a team of teachers who are excited and passionate about the trauma-informed model. Have them work with you to organize the training and have them be the "cheerleaders" for this model to help build a positive acceptance of this change. Have this team of teachers create and lead learning activities to teach the trauma-informed model. This sends a strong message to staff that this is not a top down mandate.

New Student Registration—Coming to a new school can be intimidating and scary for both the parents and students. Give them "the red carpet treatment" to help calm their anxiety and experience the "you are important to us" culture, from the minute they enter into your school. On the following page are ways this can be done:

"You never get a second chance to make a first impression."
– Will Rogers

- The receptionist or secretary should welcome every family that comes to the front counter. This person will set the first impression.

- When parents come to register their student, have the enrollment packets already put together with clipboards and a comfortable place for parents to sit and fill them out. Have pens available and signs that say, "Welcome to [Your School Name]. We're glad you're here!"

- Offer assistance to the parents if they have any difficulty with the forms. If they say they don't need help, you may want to check in with them once they start going through the paperwork, just to make sure.

- Make a special point to ask students what school they are coming from so you can make sure you are able to request their transcripts. Ask students if there are any other schools that they have attended so you can make sure that you find all of the credits they have earned. This demonstrates to the parent and student that you are willing to go the extra mile for them.

- Have coffee or water available. Ask parents if you can get them a cup of coffee or glass of water...it is a welcoming gesture that says, "We care."

- Sometimes parents will come in already charged up, defensive, or ready for a fight due to how they've been treated in the past from other schools. They can be rude and angry, so this is a great opportunity to practice the model with them in that moment. Take the high road...give them empathy. Connect with their pain. Connect with their heart. Give them love and you will see them de-escalate.

"Those who are nurtured best, survive best."
– Louis Cozolino

Build Relationships—There is no better way to begin building caring and authentic relationships than by meeting with each and every new student and their parents before they start school. This may need to be a shared responsibility due to the number of students but it sends the message that "your student may be one of many but he/she is very important to us." It reinforces the school culture you are building and conveying to the students, their parents, and the community.

Whoever meets with the parent(s) and student, instead of having the office assistant bring them to your office, go out and introduce yourself and invite them into your office. Students and parents should be given a warm welcome once you have them in your office. Share with them the positives about your school and let them know how much you appreciate them coming in with their child.

This conference is a great opportunity to share your commitment to your students, staff, and parent community as well as the following:

- Reinforce the trauma-informed culture by your words, actions, and deeds. Words such as, "You are the reason why I come to work everyday...your well-being and success are my top priority." This expresses a warm welcome and how committed you are to the student's success and engagement in the learning environment.

- Share how important it is to you that every student feels respected and valued.

- Share your commitment that every student who walks through the school doors should feel that safety is always first. Let the student know that you are just as committed to him/her as to everyone else regarding this issue.

- Let the parent(s) know that you are much stronger as a team and that you have an open door policy. If they ever want to come in with any concerns about their son/daughter, they are welcome to schedule a conference at any time to discuss any information that would be helpful to the success of their child.

- Emphasize how important it is to you that all students be successful in their classes so they are well prepared for their next grade level or transition into middle school, high school, or graduation from high school.

- If you are aware of any red flags, this is the time to address your concerns. It provides you an opportunity to begin to build the relationship by being proactive.

- If there is a history of poor attendance, ask the student to share why they have had a difficult time with attendance at the school they are coming from.

- Share with the student that you are very aggressive with attendance because you care so much about each student's school success.

- Let them know that you care so much that your team will come out to their house to pick them up and bring them to school if they are not making the effort to get to school.

- If there are behavioral issues that need to be addressed, ask the student (and parent) to share with you their experience

"A child who goes through trauma becomes concrete and rigid in his cognitive abilities because thinking in terms of life and death allows for no gray areas. It creates a sense of safety."
– Heather T. Forbes, LCSW

at their previous school. Ask them to share why they think they had discipline challenges.

- Ask them how they think discipline will be different at your school. Explain to them how your school will be different.

- Take the time to share your expectations, but phrase them in a manner that says, "I care too much about you and the other students to allow any major disruption to take away from our caring school environment."

Student Ambassadors—One of the best ways to welcome students and create an uplifting and strong school culture is to have a group of identified student ambassadors. You can either have a formal selection process or informally identify students you feel would be great representatives of your school. Have these students be an active part of giving school tours and welcoming new students.

Let these "experts" promote your school culture and do the welcoming. Peer to peer interactions can be golden. Having student ambassadors talk about their positive experiences at your school and express how much they love their school and how much their school means to them is, as they say, priceless.

Gang Involvement—If a student is coming to your school and you are aware that they have a gang affiliation or a history of gang infractions at their previous school, use this conference to address it:

- Be upfront and open. Share that you are aware that there has been some gang infractions from their previous school and ask the student to share with you how their gang affiliation will be different at your school. Help them work through solutions and strategies on how to handle any tension that might begin to build up at school. Talk through how they should handle gang issues without causing a disruption that could result in an arrest or school discipline.

- Let them know they will be treated with respect and that you expect them to be respectful by leaving their colors out on the curb before coming on school grounds.

- Let them know if gang behavior comes on school grounds that it won't be tolerated. Make it clear to them that it is disrespectful and that you have very high standards for keeping the school safe for all students, including them.

- Take the time to let the student know that you care about them and that you want them at your school. Get to the heart of the matter and let them know you would be very disappointed if they brought any gang behavior on campus.

- It is very important that you assure the student that you will protect their name if they come to you with concerns. Give them a way to communicate and without being burdened with the code of silence.

    For example, if you have security cameras, share with the student that all they have to do is walk by you and say, "Science room hallway." You'll check the cameras and observe what took place. If you have to call a student in, you tell the student you were looking at the cameras and noticed the tension or the bump of shoulders. Have your SRO sit in on these conversations. If it is a serious infraction, then you or the SRO might need to take action to reinforce your expectations that the gang issues stay out of school.

All School Kick-Off Event—Either the week before school starts or at your normal open house, invite all your new students and their families to a BBQ or similar event.

- During the event, meet in the gym or auditorium with all of the parents/students and welcome them back to your school. Introduce the teachers and acknowledge that the teachers and the entire school staff are here to be of service to the students.

- Take the time to go over your commitment to safety, your belief that each student deserves to be respected and valued, and your promise that each student's success in school will be held as a top priority.

- Take this opportunity to share how serious you take student attendance—that you care too much for your students to not have them in school.

- Have school counselors talk about student schedules.

- Have staff and student ambassadors available to mingle with the new parents and students..

- Offer an alternative to this event for students who may need a different format. Some students with a history of trauma may find such an event too overwhelming. For these students, invite them to come to the school the week before school begins to meet their teacher(s). This allows them a positive experience while the school is calm and it gives them some initial one-on-one time with their teachers. Principals may even offer to give students a personal tour of the school. This can be an effective way to start building the level of trust with a student and those in authority (typically a strong trigger for our Billys—having someone in charge of them).

Catching Up on Credits

For high school students, you may find that they are seriously behind on the required credits to graduate within a reasonable amount of time. Students impacted by trauma get overwhelmed easily and the shortage of credits will likely discourage them from even attending school. You don't want to lose these students; dropping out of school will only lead to a future of failure. Here are some creative ways to help students catch-up on their credit load:

- Provide after school programs that can provide credit hours.

- Have a seven-period day. This allows students to pick up two classes each year.

- Run summer school. Students can pick up two classes during summer school session.

- Track hours for counseling and group sessions. Apply this time as an elective credit.

- Offer self-paced classes. Under the supervision of a certified teacher, allow the student to move at his/her own pace to complete semester classes, shortening the time to complete the course.

- Give a PE credit if they participate in a sport. Work with the coach to track the student's attendance at practices and games.

- Offer an art elective for participating in a music or drama program after school. Assign an adult to document hours so they are equivalent to a quarter credit or semester credit.

Be as creative as you can but still maintain the credibility for credits earned. When an overwhelmed Billy can see that he is moving forward, he will begin to have hope.

Build Awareness—Visual reminders can speak volumes to the culture of your school. As much as interactions and relationships are important, posters that reinforce this message can also be helpful to build and maintain the awareness of your core values. Place these posters in the:

- Main office
- Principal's office
- Counselors' office
- Lunch room
- Main Hallways

Encourage teachers to also include similar posters in their classrooms.

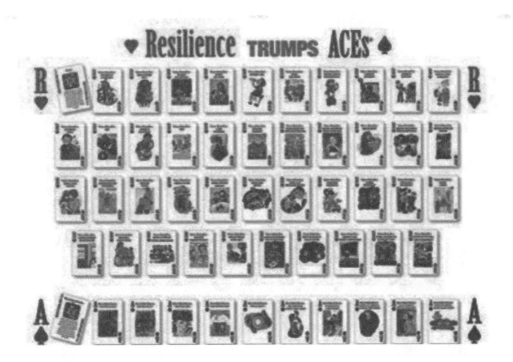

"Under the Stairs"

ELEMENTARY SCHOOL
BY JIM SPORLEDER

I was doing a school consultation with a colleague of mine. We were at an elementary school that worked from a very punitive framework.

The administration wanted us to observe a kindergartener. They said we would immediately know which one she was in the classroom without even having to point her out to us. Billy was described to us as the student who was the disruptor—who refused to adhere to the rules. She was the noncompliant student.

Before we could go into the classroom to do our observation, the class was already lined up and coming through the hallway to go to music. Billy had just run out of the classroom and was underneath the stairs, refusing to come out. The teacher was holding a strong line, telling the girl the class was going to leave without her, hoping that would be enough to sway her. But it wasn't, so the paraeducator was sent to get her out while the rest of the class went on to music.

When we came over to the stairs, the para looked at my colleague and said, "Can you help?" My colleague crawled under the stairs, reassuring the little girl saying, "You're not in trouble. I just want to be with you. You found a nice safe spot and I'd love to join you."

She started talking to her and Billy began opening up to her. Billy told my colleague that she was hiding underneath the stairs because in order to go to music, she had to walk by the first grade classroom. And Billy had been held back. She didn't want her friends to see her.

Not only was this part of the core issue driving the "defiance," my colleague found out from Billy that her mother was in jail and all her siblings were separated, living with different relatives.

Billy told my colleague, "I miss my mommy. And I miss my brothers and sisters."

This story shows that the issue at hand isn't ever the real issue. Ask the questions, "What is driving Billy's behavior?" and "What can I do at this very moment to build relationship with Billy?" and you'll be able to help students in a whole new way.

CHAPTER FIFTEEN

Step-By-Step

The following is a step-by-step checklist to use when fully implementing the trauma-informed model into your school. Use this checklist to ensure you are doing everything you need to do to have a successful first year of full implementation.

August or September—The following are suggested targets and actions to be completed the first month of school:

☐ TEACH STUDENTS ABOUT STRESS.

- Have mini-lessons prepared for teachers the first week of school to introduce to the students how stress impacts learning and behavior. For secondary schools, assign this task to the first period teachers.

- Go over the procedures with the class to explain all the options for when students are struggling and need help regulating.

- Be proactive and teach students there are options if they communicate that they are feeling a high level of stress.

- Share and fully explain the *Stress Indicator Form* (See the Appendix) with students. Again, for secondary schools, assign this task to the first period teachers.

- Take this opportunity to share with the students how the *Stress Indicator Form* works to help them identify their stress levels.

- Explain that teachers do not want to overwhelm the students or send students into the red zone where they will shut down or explode.

• Share options for when students feel completely dysregulated. Talk about proactive choices they can make before they go into the red zone and how to ask for help from the teacher. Reinforce that they "are not in trouble" when they do this and in fact, it is encouraged and a positive proactive step to take. The teacher must convey how this is a safe option and that by asking for help, they will not be perceived as failures.

• Have the teachers visually show and explain the Window of Stress Tolerance (See *Help for Billy*, Chapter 2) to your students using the Window of Stress Tolerance Worksheet in the Appendix. This is a visual learning tool even the youngest of our children can understand. Give examples of how you have approached your window of stress tolerance in the past (give personal yet appropriate examples the students can relate to). Have the students share and discuss their examples. For elementary school students, using a storybook with a character who gets easily frustrated can be a poignant way to explain this concept.

☐ TEACH PARENTS ABOUT STRESS.

There is tremendous value in having consistency in both the home and school environments. When children and adolescents live and go to school in environments that have the same standards, rules, and expectations, they thrive. This is especially true for our Billys who have difficulty transitioning and have very concrete and literal thinking patterns.

Offer parenting classes to help parents understand the impact that trauma has on children and adolescents. While this is an ideal way of bridging the gap between home and school, the reality is that getting parents to attend and participate in parenting classes is extremely difficult. Sometimes offering incentives like pizza or vouchers can be helpful.

Have your school social worker set a date for your first parent training night. Schools can be too intimidating for parents so look into the possibility of having the parent trainings at a neutral site, off of school grounds. Recruit the help of any volunteer groups you may have at the school like the PTA to market the event and bring about awareness. Recommended resources for parent materials that follow this model can be found at www.BeyondConsequences.com.

"A parent's ACE score doesn't have to be passed onto the child, but it most often does without some form of intervention."

– Jeannette Pai-Espinosa

If it becomes too challenging to get parents to attend, reach out to community partners who teach mandated parenting courses. When families get involved with the court system, parenting courses are often required. Collaborate with the agencies providing these trainings to ensure their curriculums are based off a trauma-informed paradigm.

☐ CREATE A CULTURE OF SAFETY.

Develop a classroom culture where students feel comfortable identifying their stress levels. Encourage students to express themselves emotionally. Develop regulatory strategies to handle stressful days before they become difficult behavioral days.

☐ BEGIN STUDENTS OF CONCERN (SOC) MEETINGS.

Schedule your first Students of Concern meeting with staff after the first two weeks of school. Students in need of support and assistance will begin to surface. Encourage staff to stay aware of any students that should be added to the SOC. Remind staff to fill out the appropriate form as described in Chapter 9 throughout these first couple of weeks. You might want to organize the SOC meetings into grade level meetings, depending on the size of your school.

When students are identified, ask if a staff member is connecting with these students even before you have your first kick-off SOC meeting. If not, ask if there is a volunteer who can make it a priority to connect with the student every day. To provide continuity, be sure to write this budding relationship into the action plan on the SOC document.

☐ CREATE BOOK STUDY GROUPS.

One of the best ways to learn, digest, and apply this information is through reading *Help for Billy* in a study group. Using the *Study Guide* that accompanies the *Help for Billy* book, break your staff up into small groups. Each of the groups is to be led by one of the members of the Leadership Team. Each Leadership Team member organizes and conducts his/her study group and is charged with creating an emotionally safe and comfortable atmosphere so every individual in the study group has the opportunity to dive into this material at a deep

"Many abused children cling to the hope that growing up will bring escape and freedom."
– Judith Lewis Herman

personal level. The leader should encourage the group to discuss each topic covered in the book at an in-depth and meaningful level. The leader is also charged to keep each meeting on track and on task.

Ideally, these study groups should meet once a week or once every two weeks. However, this may have to be adjusted as needed with the realities of your school day and the requirements placed on your teachers.

☐ Encourage Staff at Staff Meetings.

Teachers will find this model extremely difficult at first and will want to give up and go back to their familiar traditional ways. Here are two ways to encourage your staff:

- Have staff share their recent success stories. Many times it only takes a small shift to see huge results so be sure to highlight these moments of brilliance to help build the momentum.

- As an administrator, share how the discipline is going in your office and the results you are seeing. Share stories of how you've been able to directly correlate students' stress with their behaviors. Help your staff to understand that by asking the question, "What is driving this behavior?" you have been able to help students and reduce behavioral outbursts.

☐ Repeat, Repeat, Repeat.

Keep the message in front of your staff. The more you have staff consistently connecting with students, the "village" of support will strengthen and build. This will help more students improve their ability to stay regulated, handle stress, and build resilience skills.

"Tell me and I'll forget. Show me and I may remember. Involve me and I learn."

– Benjamin Franklin

Each adult relationship has the potential to change a life path and school staff needs to be reminded of how important they are to the implementation process. The more adults connected to your students (especially the most difficult Billys at your school), the more they build their village of support. This is a game changer! Your school plays a huge role in the lives of the students who come into your classrooms.

So keep reminding and encouraging staff until it becomes second nature to them. One of the best ways to implement change is to create new habits. It takes repetition, repetition, repetition.

October—By October, if not earlier, you should be able to feel and see the culture starting to reflect the trauma-informed model. There will be examples to share with staff about meaningful conversations with students, so allocate time at staff meetings to allow staff to share the successes they are experiencing.

The following is a checklist of suggested targets and actions to be completed for October:

☐ STAFF SURVEY.

At the beginning of October, have all your staff complete the *Staff Survey* (see the Appendix). There should be two surveys completed: one now and one towards the end of the school year in April or May. Giving two surveys will help you see the changes that are going to take place this school year, and they will guide you in your journey forward with this model. The survey can be done with copies of the survey on paper, however it is strongly encouraged to do the survey using an electronic online program such as Survey Monkey[1] or Google Forms. Using an online survey allows you to easily tally up the results and be able to store them in electronic form for reference in the coming months and years.

☐ STUDENT CLIMATE SURVEY.

Also at the beginning of October, you'll want to administer the *Student Climate Survey* (see the Appendix) so you can measure how this program is changing the hearts and minds of your students. As with the *Staff Survey*, you'll want to give this survey in early October and towards the end of the school year in April or May. Here are the suggested steps to follow for this important survey:

○ CREATE A STUDENT CLIMATE SURVEY COMMITTEE.
Develop a committee to assess whether the *Student Climate Survey* included in this administrative guide (see the Appendix) is asking the information that fits your students and the vulnerability of their trauma. This committee should be a good representation of the teachers in your school.

> *"Numerous scientific studies have documented and supported the risks and predictable negative behavioral outcomes that derive from inadequate maternal/infant bonding and attunement."*
> —Dr. Robert Scaer

"The toughest thing about the power of trust is that it's very difficult to build and very easy to destroy."

– Thomas J. Watson

The *Student Climate Survey* was developed to determine the areas in which your students are struggling. It is designed to provide specific information about where your students need the most support. It is also designed to assist you in developing programs or resources to meet the challenging issues that your students are facing.

Have the committee look over the survey to see if they are comfortable with the questions on the survey or if there are other questions they would like added. Only make changes if you have a majority of committee members agreeing on the proposed changes.

Create the survey on Survey Monkey or Google Forms. These electronic programs can also do all the analysis.

DEVELOP A PLAN FOR THE STUDENT CLIMATE SURVEY. Choose a sampling of all grade levels in your school. It might be easiest to plan to administer the survey in the health or P.E. classes to get a good sampling of all the different students.

Many of the questions on the survey are sensitive in nature so it is advised that you send either a note home or you program an automated phone call to the parents to let them know you will be administering the test. Let them know it will be anonymous but if they would like to have their child opt out of the survey, they can call the front office, no questions asked. Be sure to check your district policy on administering the survey to stay within the guidelines.

ADMINISTER THE STUDENT CLIMATE SURVEY. When administering the survey, create as much safety around the survey so you get honest results. Make it clear to your students that the survey results are anonymous. Let the students know they can opt out of taking the survey or opt out of any questions they are not comfortable answering.

Explain that the survey is a tool for making sure that you can provide the best services for them. Explain that it is a non-judgmental survey that allows you to get a better perspective on what they are going through and to develop programs or support systems that meet the needs that are revealed in the survey results. Bottom line: it is a survey to help you understand and "know" them.

☐ MAIN OFFICE.

The main office should be working as a team. Parents should feel a welcoming climate when they come in the office to meet for appointments, to communicate with the office, or register a new student. If the paradigm shift isn't evident in the main office, you may be building the model on weak ground.

☐ COMMUNITY PARTNERS.

Connections with community partners should be established and those partners should be coming into the school to provide services. Keep building your referral list of what agencies provide what services in your community.

☐ SOC MEETINGS.

The SOC meetings should be productive and staff should be able to see the action plans taking place as they are developed.

☐ IMPROVED WELL-BEING OF STUDENTS.

Students should be responding to the outreach of staff and the new approach to school discipline.

☐ STAFF IMPLEMENTATION.

You should begin to see consistency with your staff's implementation. A supportive approach with your encouragement should be enough to get all your staff on board but if this is not working with some resistant staff, you should have initiated some very direct conversations. By this point you will have student examples to indicate how the staff member is not bonding with students. Students are typically very honest and open...they will let you know which teachers are setting them off. You will be able to see patterns of how some teachers continue to deal with the students in harsh and punitive ways. For example, some students will be able to take responsibility for their actions, owning the fact that they were out of line but at the same time, they will let you know that it was the teacher's reactivity that worsened the situation until they lost it.

"Trauma has a two-fold potential; it can be the catalyst for creative change or the cause of self-destruction."
–John Bradshaw

☐ PROVIDE FEEDBACK.

As an administrator, your encouragement and support for your staff at an individual level is going to be critical at this stage. Provide feedback to staff members by doing mini-observations in their classrooms and in their interactions with students around the school. Emphasize to your staff that there will be different styles that match one's personality and that is fine, as long as everyone is heading toward the same goal of building caring adult relationships with students. Let them know what you observe in their classrooms and help them to see that implementing these strategies is impacting student behavior and learning in a positive way.

> *"What the teacher is, is more important than what he teaches."*
>
> *– Karl Menninger*

- Leave a brief note on the teacher's desk after you have done a mini-walk-through and observation to share something positive with the teacher.
- Get out and encourage the model and remember that every school will move at a different pace. As long as you can see that you are moving forward, celebrate your progress.

November—By November, you should be in full implementation and seeing the results of your commitment. You will be able to see the culture of your school becoming much more connected.

The following is a checklist of to be completed for November:

☐ COMPLETE A SELF-EVALUATION.

Ask yourself the following questions and be as objective as possible to get an honest gauge on how this is unfolding in your school. You are going to be further along in some areas than others. Celebrate your successes and strengthen those areas that you feel need help.

• What are you seeing in the office when students are referred?

_____

_____

_____

_____

• How is the *Stress Indicator Form* working now that you have had a couple of months to implement it into the conversations you are having with students?

_____

_____

_____

_____

• How are students responding to learning about stress and the impact it has on their brains and their ability to learn?

_____

_____

_____

_____

• Has the *Stress Indicator Form* been a productive tool? Can you share specific incidents with staff where the stress form deepened your conversation with one or more of your students?

_____

_____

_____

_____

• What evidence can you identify that the staff is using the implementation strategies?

_____

_____

_____

_____

"Giving and receiving unconditional love is the most effective and powerful way to personal wholeness and happiness."
–John Bradshaw

- What are some of the identifiable advantages to having a small group welcoming the students as they come on campus in the morning?

_____
_____
_____
_____

"Everyone has an invisible sign hanging from their neck saying, 'Make me feel important.' Never forget this message when working with people."

– Mary Kay Ash

- What changes have you seen by having a person in the cafeteria greeting students at breakfast and lunch?

_____
_____
_____
_____

- What evidence can you identify that positive interventions and relationships are happening as you have staff present after school wishing the students a safe and good afternoon?

_____
_____
_____
_____

- Are you using these opportunities to observe and look for opportunities to let specific students know how much you appreciate their behavior, attendance, or getting to know them better?

_____
_____
_____
_____

- Is staff using the SOC protocol appropriately? Are they able to see interventions and action plans in progress?

_____
_____
_____
_____

• What is the feeling in the main office when visitors walk through the front door? Is a trauma-informed culture being created that is warm, welcoming, and inclusive?

_____

_____

_____

_____

☐ School Resource Officer.

The SRO should be in a consistent pattern of walking the building at different times during the class periods. He should be present during passing time, interacting with student and building relationships so students can begin trusting and seeking help from the SRO when needed. The SRO should be participating in the conversation in the office in which you are taking a proactive approach. Also, the SRO should be an important and integrated member of your office team by now. He should be building positive relationships with the students. If the SRO is undermining your work in any way, you need to address this immediately. The SRO cannot be a barrier for students who would otherwise come into the office seeking help.

January—By January, you are half way through your first full year of implementing a trauma-informed school. There is still work to be done but the hurdle of starting the process is behind you! Stay strong and go through the following checklist of suggested targets and actions:

☐ Review Disciplinary Stats.

Look at your _Behavior Tracker_ and see if you can draw some conclusion as to how the implementation of the trauma-informed model has impacted office referrals for discipline. Review the following:

• Out-of-school suspensions

• Emergency expulsions

• Expulsions

• Number of students referred to the office for discipline

• Arrests or charges at school by the SRO

☐ REVIEW ATTENDANCE DATA.

Look at your attendance data and see how they compare to the last couple of years. For the students identified on your SOC list, see if you have been able to positively impact their attendance through SOC meetings and action plans.

☐ CHECK STUDENT GRADES.

- How are the overall grades of your students now compared to the same time last year and the year before?

_____

_____

_____

_____

- For students who were failing, are they now improving their grades and earning their credits?

_____

_____

_____

_____

"If one does not know to which port one is sailing, no wind is favorable."

– Lucius Annaeus Seneca

- Do you have a plan in place to help students who are deficient in credits and are students using it?

_____

_____

_____

_____

☐ RATE YOUR OVERALL IMPLEMENTATION.

- On a scale of 1 to 10 (in which a higher score is better), where would you place your school in the implementation process?

1   2   3   4   5   6   7   8   9   10

• Is this score higher than when you started the year off? Why or why not?

_____

_____

_____

_____

• On a scale of 1 to 10, how would you rate your students' understanding of how, without interventions, ACEs can hinder their lives?

        1   2   3   4   5   6   7   8   9   10

"There are no secrets to success. It is the result of preparation, hard work, and learning from failure."

– Colin Powell

• On a scale of 1 to 10, how many of your students by now can give you feedback on their knowledge of how to trump the ACEs in their lives?'

        1   2   3   4   5   6   7   8   9   10

• On a scale of 1 to 10, where do your staff see themselves with the implementation process?'

        1   2   3   4   5   6   7   8   9   10

• On a scale of 1 to 10, is your office discipline showing progress and are referrals dropping?

        1   2   3   4   5   6   7   8   9   10

• On a scale of 1 to 10, how is your ISS and/or Safe Rooms working?

        1   2   3   4   5   6   7   8   9   10

• Do any adjustments need to be made?

_____

_____

_____

_____

• On a scale of 1 to 10, how are you doing with the book study groups?

1   2   3   4   5   6   7   8   9   10

• On a scale of 1 to 10, how are you doing with your professional development? Are you hitting the mark?

1   2   3   4   5   6   7   8   9   10

Having low scores is not bad; it is an indicator that you need to focus on areas that you feel best meet the needs of your students. This is a process that takes time; you aren't going to see significant changes in staff until they gain a greater understanding of how to work with students dealing with toxic stress. Your staff is on a new journey; they are developing new tools for their toolboxes and they are developing meaningful and caring relationships with their students. Trust the process.

> *"I believe that every single event in life happens in an opportunity to choose love over fear."*
> *– Oprah Winfrey*

February—If you live in a cold climate, by February you're probably feeling the effects of winter on the morale of your staff and students. This is more reason to stay connected and to do all you can at the relationship level to keep up the momentum. Here is a checklist to be completed for February:

☐ FOCUS ON YOUR STUDENTS OF CONCERN (SOC).

Be very consistent in scheduling the SOC meetings because they encourage feedback, which in turn creates action. Self-check to make sure your action plans are proactive and work at improving any concerns brought up by staff. Hold staff accountable for filling out the forms and turning them into the person you put in charge of running the SOC meetings. This saves time, gets right to the point, and prevents staff members who do not fill out the forms from dominating the meetings.

It is critical that action plans be completed and documented so that staff is aware of the interventions and progress. If a student's name comes up continually, then the administration may need to have a parent conference and be progressive with each action plan. Seek parent feedback on how to solve the problem; this is not normally done in our system but it can be an extremely effective way to solve the issues at hand.

☐ KEEP BUILDING RELATIONSHIPS.

Your daily practice of being highly visible to students and staff during the day will have a significant impact on the school culture and climate. When relationships are made outside the office, it helps to sooth the tension when a student is referred to the office. If Billy has at least a small amount of trust in you, it makes problem-solving with him easier and he will be more apt to disclose and identify the core cause of the problem.

"A smile is the beginning of peace."
– Mother Teresa

The most effective strategy to helping a student trump his or her ACEs is relationship, relationship, relationship! This cannot be emphasized enough. Students impacted by trauma are hungry for caring adult relationships that are stable, consistent, and unconditionally accepting. This is a skill that you and your staff will develop and improve as your understanding of trauma and toxic stress impacts the way you approach your students.

March, April, and May—With only a few more months of school left in the year, you'll want to do some assessments to evaluate how far you've come and where you still need to go. This will also help in your planning for the next school year. Here is a checklist to be completed for the coming months:

☐ RE-ADMINISTER THE *STAFF SURVEY*.

Using the same survey you gave in October to your staff, give it again to your staff in April or May. This will be your post-test.

After compiling the results of both the October survey and this end-of-year survey, identify what has been successful with the staff this first year of full implementation and what areas still need to be refined. Identify your target areas and use them for your plan of action for the next school year.

These first-year comparative results should give you a road map for what you need for the second year of implementation. Collectively as a school, you'll also be able to identify areas to provide more in-depth professional development around trauma.

☐ RE-ADMINISTER THE *STUDENT CLIMATE SURVEY*.

Using the same survey you gave to your students at the beginning of October, administer it using the same protocol as before in April or May.

After compiling the results of both the October survey and this end-of-year survey, identify what has been successful this first year of full implementation and what areas still need to be refined. Share the results with the Leadership Team and create a plan for how to make the next school year even better.

At your discretion, share with those at your school and the community partners who could benefit from this survey information. It should be on a "need to know basis only." For example, at Lincoln High school, student results were shared with the Lincoln Health Center so they could make sure their services aligned with the needs of the students in the survey results.

☐ EVALUATE YOUR TARGET AREAS.

From both the *Staff Survey* and the *Student Climate Survey*, identify your target areas. Identify what was going well and what needs further development for the next school year. Spend your energy on the recommended targets, and think twice about putting anything else on your plate at this time. This is a process and it will take chopping it up into phases.

☐ IDENTIFY TRAINING NEEDS.

For the next school year, identify the areas to focus on for the August staff training days. What areas are needed for your staff to develop a deeper understanding? Pull from your *Staff Survey* results. Create a plan of action now to develop this training so you are well-prepared by August.

Throughout the School Year. The following are tasks that should be continued each month throughout the entire school year:

- Keep having different staff members share their success stories using trauma-informed strategies.

- Staff should be meeting in their book study groups and working through the material to comprehend this information at a more in-depth level.

- The administration has to be proactive about having conversations with staff who are pushing back on the new approach throughout the school year. Keep on top of this in order to support the school mission.

- As you move through the school year, you should be able to see lower numbers of referrals coming into the office. Be sure to compliment staff on how well they are connecting with students, especially those connecting with the most challenging of students.

- Office staff should give periodic updates on how they are using the *Stress Indicator Form* when students come into the office. Open up the discussion of how to better use this tool and how to make sure it is giving students the opportunity to identify their stress levels.

- Home visits should continue throughout the year for those students who are struggling with attendance. Have a strong support person to assist and help with this challenge.

- Continue to allocate time during staff meetings to have staff share the positive difference they are seeing this year compared to previous years.

- SOC meetings should be going smoothly. They should be productive and action plans should be carried out without delay. The action plans should be making a significant difference for these students. By using this SOC intervention system, you are giving the message to everyone, "this is how we take care of our kids."

- Professional development days should be scheduled throughout the year.

- Continually check to make sure the attendance policy is being followed and that it is productive.

- Continually check quarterly and semester grades. Identify the students who have struggled in the past, and look to see how their grades or progress have improved.

- Throughout the year, monitor the implementation process and record your observations.

- As busy as you are, one of your most important tasks is the need to continually oversee the documentation of all the data—from survey results to student attendance to student grades. Be sure that time is allotted to properly assemble and save this data so you have a baseline comparison for next year and the years to follow.

- Develop and sustain good relationships with your community partners. They have excellent resources so you'll want to be aware of what specific resources they have available and how to best collaborate with them. Some community resource examples include the following: the local food bank, domestic violence shelters, Good Will, Salvation Army, Juvenile Justice Department, Children's Home Society (and other non-profit family oriented agencies), and faith-based community organizations (churches, synagogues , temples, etc.). These organizations are critical for supporting your students and their families. For instance, if you have a student whose family had their electricity turned off and need help getting it turned back on, do you know who you would turn to?

- And always ask yourself this question, **"What does the staff need to sustain the momentum?"** throughout the entire year.

June—Congratulations, you have just completed your first year of implementation of the trauma-informed model!

As you look back at the start of your journey, you will most likely be able to see that you have had encouraging growth and have seen a significant change in your students within the family culture that you have developed. The meaningful conversations and caring relationships you have developed with your students should be the driving force to learn more about trauma and to continue on this journey of helping students not just "behave" but "heal."

The following are examples of ways you will know your efforts have been effective and well worth the time, energy, and dedication:

- A reduction in office referrals for student discipline.

- A reduction in the number of days students are sent home from school for behavioral issues.

- A change in your staff's attitude and overall morale as evidenced by the staff pre- and post-surveys.

- An increase in your students' ability to self-regulate within a trauma-informed environment.

- An increase in the ability of your students to grow academically because of their increase in feeling safe as well as their emotional and social needs being met.

- A positive change in your school climate due to the improved ability of the staff to interact, support, and engage with the students.

Hopefully you are feeling excited for your students, staff, and support team as you step out and lead this movement to educate your community about the impact trauma has on all of us. Implementing this process throughout our K-12 educational programs will provide a common language and vocabulary that can be shared across grade levels, as well as transitions from elementary to middle school and then on to high school. Your school will become the leader that others will want to follow. You will become the teacher of teachers, with influence that reaches beyond your district and across the country.

The authors truly believe this is what lies ahead for you as you have demonstrated the courage to make a difference in the lives of your students, who have had little to no control or choice over the trauma journey they have been on and continue to be on. You are teaching them the resiliency they need in order to overcome and learn the resiliency skills that will "trump" their ACEs and "trump" their trauma.

Can you think of a greater gift that you can give your students than the gift of hope and the path to become the special individual they were meant to be?

"Never doubt that a small group of thoughtful citizens can change the world. Indeed it is the only thing that ever has."
– Margaret Mead

"Can You Please Help Me? "

ELEMENTARY SCHOOL
BY JIM SPORLEDER

I was asked to observe a first grade classroom with two students that had to be removed from class almost daily. It was my first time going into this classroom and I knew it was important for me to connect with the kids by getting down on one knee so that my size wasn't intimidating. I also knew it was important for me to start connecting with all the other students; I didn't want the two students I was observing to think I was only there to observe them. As soon as I walked into the classroom, the teacher stopped her lesson and walked over to me. She used her head to try and point out which students I was to be observing—her "disruptive" students. She shared with me in a voice tone that others could hear, "This class is very hard to teach and many of them are out of control."

There were 18 students and two paraeducators in the room with the teacher. I began working my way around the room and building a rapport with the students. At one table, a paraeducator was sitting at the table with a group of students but she was not interacting in a positive manner. She was barking out at students that were not on task. As I looked at the table with the two students I was to observe, there was a paraeducator standing five feet from the table with his arms crossed and again, having no interaction with any of the students. The closer I got to the table, one of the students was sitting backwards in his chair, making noises, and had not started on the learning activity. The paraeducator did not move in to interact with the students or with the boy who was already disengaged in the learning activity.

I finally worked my way to the boy and I asked him if he could share with me about his family and how many brothers and sisters he had.

He immediately started to share and we had a positive conversation. I finally asked him if he could teach me how to do the assignment that he had been avoiding. He spun around in his chair and explained what they were supposed to be doing. I asked him if he could show me so that I would be able to do the assignment with him. He began explaining the assignment as he was working. I stayed with him until I knew he was well on his way to completing the activity. As I walked toward the other student, she looked up at me and said, "Can you please help me? I do not understand what I am suppose to do." I knelt down and began asking questions that I knew she would be able to answer and then we were prepared for the learning activity. I stayed with her until I knew she was confident and would be successful. As I was leaving the classroom, the little boy was pulling at my shirt...he wanted me to see his finished assignment.

Too many times, we create our own problems and we label students without any interventions or observations to see where they are emotionally. In one classroom, we had three missed opportunities to provide support and safety:

1. The teacher was keeping her distance from the students and had labeled the class as difficult and unteachable.

2. The paraeducator only communicated through confrontation and reactivity instead of connection and support.

3. The other paraeducator was physically positioned five feet from the table where the two most challenging students sat, initiating no interaction with either of them or the other students in the classroom.

We create our own problems when we are not proactive by providing positive caring adult relationships. It takes interacting with our students in a positive way. If our only interaction is correction at a distance, then we create classrooms that are not safe, we trigger students, and we miss opportunities to build resiliency through relationship.

As adults, we have to be the ones who gain a greater understanding of our students so that we can provide the culture of safety and nurturing. If we are going to stand back and then react to a problem, we set the student up for failure and take away any sense of safety or feeling loved. As a stranger in this classroom, I was immediately able to build a rapport with the two most challenging students. I was able to meet their need for safety and take their fear of failure away through simple interactions of empathy and connectedness.

PART THREE

Strategies

CHAPTER SIXTEEN

Relationship Strategies

No matter the age of your students, the basic strategy for relating to them will be the same. In fact, you can use the relationship strategies presented in this guide on anyone—your spouse or partner, your pesky neighbor, or even your in-laws and outlaws.

Seriously, the strategies in this guide and in this chapter can be used when relating to anyone who is coming from a different perspective from you and has a tendency to be reactive towards you. In schools, these strategies should be used between the following dyads:

- Principal → Student
- Teacher → Student
- Paraeducator → Student
- Receptionist → Student
- Cafeteria Worker → Student
- Janitor → Student
- Guidance Counselor → Student
- SRO → Student

As well as between:

- Principal → Teacher
- Principal → Vice-Principal
- Principal → Parent
- Principal → SRO

- Teacher → Teacher
- Teacher → Paraeducator
- Teacher → Parent
- SRO → Teacher
- *and more....*

These strategies are a way to put empathy into action to help the person you're interacting with feel validated, heard, accepted, and worthy. But most importantly, these strategies need to be used with Billy, especially the most dysregulated Billys dealing with trauma in their present lives or healing from trauma in the past. Keep these important thoughts in mind:

- Academic learning will always be one of the top goals of this model...however, no learning can take place until a student is functioning in his brain from a top-down control. Academic learning and engagement will come once we help an escalated student calm back down, when we meet the immediate need of safety, or when we remove the griping sensation that comes with the fear of failure.

- You don't always know what the student has been through the night before or that morning prior to coming to school. We also don't know what triggers the student may be experiencing from trauma in the past.

- The Billys of your schools react out of fear; it may look like anger or other misbehaviors but underneath is a deep state of fear. Instead of seeing the anger, the disrespect, the disobedience, or the non-compliance, always look for the fear.

- Be vigilant for students who become isolative in their social behaviors. These are the students who easily get overlooked but are typically the students who need the most connection, so they don't slowly fade away from school unnoticed.

- Many of our trauma-impacted students have the heavy load of carrying too many ACEs. Without the connection at school with a caring adult, these are the students who will end up dropping out. Also, many of them will find themselves involved in the criminal system with a lifetime of being in and out of prison.

"Raise your words, not your voice. It is rain that grows flowers, not thunder."

– Rumi

Respond Instead of React. The following information is also in the book, *Help for Billy,* but it bears repeating here. In the left hand column are some of the traditional reactions matched up with a new loving trauma-informed response in the right hand column.

TRADITIONAL REACTIONS	TRAUMA-INFORMED RESPONSES
" Go to the Principal's office."	"I'm here. You're not in trouble."
"Stop crying."	"It's okay to feel."
"Stop acting like a baby."	"That really set you back, didn't it?"
"Detention is waiting for you."	"Sit with me."
"Don't you talk to an adult like that."	"You're allowed to have a voice. Lets talk together."
"You're old enough to handle this on your own."	"Let's handle this together."
"Stop whining."	"I want to understand you better. If I know how you feel, I'll be able to help you better. Use your voice so I can really understand."
"It's not that difficult."	"I need to know how hard this is for you."
"You should never have acted like that."	"Sometimes life just gets too big, doesn't it?"
"Act your age."	"This is too big to keep to yourself."
"I can't help you with this issue. I've got 30 other children in the classroom."	"We'll get through this together. Every single student in this class is important."
"I'm calling your parents. Wait until they find out."	"Let's get everyone involved to support you. You're not in trouble. I want your parents involved so we can all find a way to make this better."
"Nobody is going to like you if you keep misbehaving."	"I know you want to be well liked, so let's make that happen."
"You need to take ownership."	"I'm sorry this is so hard."

A question to always ask yourself when dealing with Billy is this: **Am I responding to Billy as a person or am I reacting to his behavior?** Responding to Billy brings about change. Reacting to Billy causes fear and emotional escalation that quickly can get out of control.

Give Emotional Space. When Billy is dysregulated, he is working from a bottom-up control within his brain. That means he is highly emotional instead of logical. To connect with him when he is like this, it requires giving him "emotional space." It is imperative to give Billy emotional space at this moment so he can release the traumatic energy that is bubbling up and erupting. It is similar to a volcano...once a volcano starts to blow, you can't stop it and plug it up. Here are some ways to do this:

- Give acceptance without solving the issue.

- Ask exploratory questions to create a deeper understanding.

- Allow the student to be upset, without insisting the student stop being upset.

- Accept that the student's reality may be skewed; when he is dysregulated do not try to convince him of a different reality.

- Tolerate the negative and exaggerated feelings the student is expressing for the moment, in order to help him calm down.

- Give understanding to the student's issue but not necessarily agree with it.

- Be kind, loving, safe and patient.

- Listen with no agenda of teaching a life lesson. Simply listen. The life lesson will come afterward.

- Engage in the conversation, but do not force or insist on answers. Let it unfold naturally.

- Focus on the relationship. Strive for emotional safety and stay regulated. Trust in the process.

"Speak when you are angry – and you'll make the best speech you'll ever regret."

– Laurence J. Peter

Ask the Right Questions. One of the main reasons we have been unable to help the Billys of our schools is because we have been asking the wrong question. We have been asking, "How do I get Billy to change his behavior?" This is the wrong question because Billy's struggle isn't behaviorally based. His struggle is based in gaps in his development, past and/or present trauma, negative beliefs, lack of relationships, and dysregulation.

The new question we need to be asking is:

QUESTION #1:
"What is driving Billy's behavior?"

It may not always be obvious what is driving Billy's behavior, so these supplemental questions listed in the following table may help to uncover the core of Billy's behavior:

WHAT ELSE IS REALLY GOING ON HERE?	The behavior is a mask and a reaction to something deeper that is driving the behavior.
WHAT DOES THIS CHILD NEED?	Billy needs a safe place to go to get his emotions under control so he can problem solve. Looking at what Billy needs allows you to assess his stress level. Confrontation will only escalate the student to a new level of fear and many times to a total loss of control.
HOW CAN I CHANGE MY PERSPECTIVE?	We typically go straight to the conclusion that the student is "trying to get away" with bad behavior or something similar. Change your perspective to look through the lens of the student. Many times, what our students do makes logical sense from their perspective.
WHAT KEEPS ME ONLY LOOKING AT BEHAVIOR?	Billy has a well-developed ability to set off triggers within those who are interacting with him. If your reaction is overly exaggerated, there may be something beyond just Billy's behavior that is opening up an old wound inside of you. This is very common, so give yourself grace and let yourself see what is opening up inside of you before interacting with Billy.
WHAT IS THIS BEHAVIOR COMMUNICATING RIGHT NOW?	Behavior is a form of communication and what you see in the moment might be the building of past events. The behavior can be a reflection or outcome of a traumatic event that happened in the home that was very disturbing to the student.
WHAT IN THE ENVIRONMENT COULD BE TRIGGERING THE BEHAVIOR?	A certain word or action can set off one of Billy's triggers and have nothing to do with the classroom or the school. It just happens to expose itself while at school.

Along with this first question, you will also want to be asking this second question:

QUESTION #2
"What can I do at this very moment to improve my relationship with this student?"

Understanding how to relate to Billy in the moment takes practice and a refined level of attunement with him. Use the following additional questions to guide you in making a connection with Billy when he is dysregulated and resistant:

- How can I make this relationship safe for Billy?
- Does Billy need me to validate him?
- What does Billy need from me?
- How can I respond to Billy so he doesn't feel threatened?
- How can I physically position myself to create safety for Billy?
- Can Billy respond to exploratory questions, not solutions I give him, that show I am interested?
- How can I convince Billy that I truly want to understand his struggle?
- How can I be more authentic with Billy?
- If I stop talking and start listening, will Billy feel like he has a voice?
- How can I serve Billy?

"Where there is anger, there is always pain underneath."

– Eckhart Tolle

These are powerful questions for you to reflect on your current classroom disciplinary practices. The questions are asking how to respond to the student—not how to react to the behavior. The questions are asking you to step out of your shoes and step into the student's shoes.

Try to understand what might be setting off his emotional triggers. If a student goes home every night to a stressed-out family, he may not be receiving the safety or the nurturing environment in which he deserves to be raised. You can make a significant impact on Billy's life by building a relationship with Billy that validates him, listens to him, seeks to know what caused his trigger to go off, and provides a safe nurturing school environment.

Knowing what a student impacted by trauma needs is a powerful model of teaching resilience, problem solving, and trust. The disruption is not about you. It is about the student. When we keep our focus on the student, change begins to take place; the journey begins for that student.

The H4B Sequence—Below is a typical sequence you will want to follow when connecting with Billy who's arousal system is charged up. The "Help for Billy Sequence" or the "H4B Sequence" for short, is as follows:

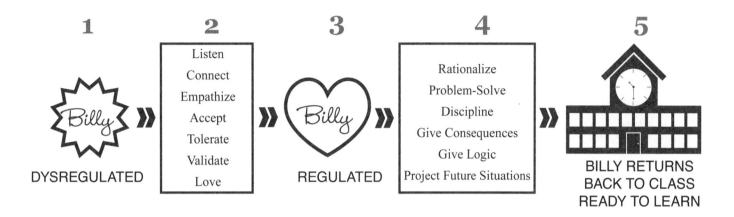

1. First, stay attuned to all your students the best you can. Staying in a proactive stance will help you to decrease the number of complete blowouts. When you notice a student becoming dysregulated, take a deep breath to regulate yourself.

2. If possible, connect with Billy, approach him in a calm voice and see if you can remove him from the situation, where there won't be an audience. Be in a receiving mode and do the following:

- LISTEN to what he is saying. Just listen…see if he is trying to tell you something about why he is upset and dysregulated. He may drop certain clues about "the real issue behind the issue." For instance, if he is upset about his hat being taken away, it may not be about the hat. He may be feeling like he is being treated unfairly and is being disrespected because another student didn't have her hat taken away. Feeling disrespected may be a huge trigger for him so the issue goes much deeper than just the hat.

"The word 'listen' contains the same letters as the word 'silent'."
– Alfred Brendel

Additionally, recognize that part of the traumatic experience involves not having a voice. Billy didn't get to have a voice during decision-making processes in the past—his perpetrators silenced him. Or, when he did speak, people didn't listen to him or told him he was lying. Thus, it is extremely important to allow Billy to have a voice during Step 2.

- CONNECT with Billy in an unconditional way. Be open to his point of view, whether right or wrong. Be present in the moment to allow yourself to get into his shoes.

- EMPATHIZE with Billy's struggle. Use phrases such as, "I'm so sorry this is so hard." or "Sometimes being a kid is really tough." Be sure to not minimize Billy's struggle. Avoid phrases that start with, "At least..." or "You shouldn't be upset about that...." or "You're overreacting...." or anything similar to these phrases. This is minimizing Billy's struggle. You'll want to maximize his struggle.

- ACCEPT that Billy is struggling and that he is angry. He very well may be overreacting or out-of-reality in his thinking. For the time being, however, just accept that his perception is his reality. Also realize that anger may be the only emotion he has ever learned. This may be a family pattern he is simply repeating in the school.

- TOLERATE For the moment, tolerate Billy's attitude, language, and non-verbal communication, such as giving you the "stink-eye," crossing his arms in a defensive posture, or rolling his eyes at you. All of this is inappropriate behavior but now is NOT the time to correct and give the life lesson. The life lesson can only be done effectively once Billy is back in his thinking brain (his neocortex). Right now, he is still in a "bottom-up control." You will have a chance to teach him and correct him soon.

- VALIDATE his ramblings and his rant. By validating him, this does not mean you are

> *"Your presence is the most precious gift you can give to another human being."*
>
> – Marshall Rosenberg

> *"The hunger for love is much more difficult to remove than the hunger for bread."*
>
> – Mother Teresa

agreeing with him. You are simply relating to his perspective of the situation. Additionally, be sure to avoid being condescending. It's not just the words you use, but the intention and feelings behind them that matter.

- LOVE him right where he is. Love is about allowing, not about trying to control, convince, or change someone. You are showing Billy what unconditional love feels like to get him back to a state of regulation.

"All bad behavior is really a request for love, attention, or validation."
— Kimberly Giles

3. Once Billy is regulated, he will be able to be more rational and logical in his thinking. Notice his body language as it will typically soften and his entire stance will be less defensive at this point. This is when Billy is coming back to a "top-down" control in his brain. You may have to "test the waters" to see if Billy is all the way calmed down or if he is still too dysregulated to talk rationally. If he begins to become reactive, simply go back to Step 2 and work to calm him down some more.

4. Now that Billy is back to a top-down control, you can begin to have the conversation turn to more logic and rational thinking. This is one of the most critical parts of the process because you want to make sure that Billy has the opportunity to learn and develop better coping skills for dealing with stress. In this step you'll want to do the following:

- Review what happened.
- Discuss how Billy could have responded instead of reacting to the situation.
- Problem-solve to find a solution to the situation.
- Talk about how Billy can make amends to the situation and to the people involved.
- Deliver any boundaries or consequences that are appropriate or needed. Be sure that you're not just punishing Billy for the sake of punishing him. This

"Listening to both sides of a story will convince you that there is more to a story than both sides."
— Frank Tyger

H4B Sequence, when followed correctly, will teach Billy how to do things differently. There really is no reason to punish a student for being dysregulated... we want to teach Billy how to stay regulated and build a strong relationship with him so he has someone to support him in this process.

Remember, the brain drives behavior. Therefore, his behavior is out of Billy's control when he is highly escalated. He cannot physiologically problem-solve, focus, or learn when his brain is overwhelmed with cortisol.

5. At this point, Billy should be ready to return to class. However, first ask him if he is ready to go back. He may need a few more minutes to be able to process what just happened. He may also need a few minutes to prepare for returning back to his classroom. If he had a major blowout in the classroom, it will take courage to go back in and face the teacher and his fellow peers. Give him five or ten minutes, if needed. If at this point, he still isn't ready, he may need you to go a bit more Patton on him by saying it is time to return to class but give him the option of either going back by himself or you walking with him so you can provide the support he may need.

"A man sooner or later discovers that he is the master-gardener of his soul, the director of his life. "

— James Allen

Sample Responses—This entire model is a very different way of relating to students than what we have traditionally done in the past. Few of us as children ourselves, ever had adults relating to us in this manner, so it truly can feel like learning a foreign language. To help guide you during conversations, several sample responses are listed below.

Read through the list on the following page and highlight or circle the ones that feel the most natural to you and try them out the next time you are interacting with a challenging student:

- "What do you need from me right now so that I can meet your need?"

- "It looks like you're having a hard day."

- "Help me to understand what's going on."

- "I know it's hard, but the more you keep it inside of you, the harder it gets."

- "You're not in trouble. We're going to work this out together."

- "I had no idea this was so hard for you!"

- "Breathe. Take a deep breath."

- "This is too much to carry all by yourself. Can you share it with me?"

- "I want to understand you better and if I know how you feel, I'll be able to do what you need me to do."

- "I believe in you, no matter what happened."

- "Give yourself permission to have a voice. I'm listening."

- "I remember when I was a little girl/boy and a friend of mine was really mean to me...." (Relate a story of yours to help a student feel connected.)

- "You have every right to be angry."

- "I get it...this really isn't fair, is it?"

- "I'm sorry this is so hard for you."

- "School really isn't working for you, is it? Tell me more...."

- "I can see you're very upset and I'm struggling, also. What can I do for you so we can both get back on track?"

- "_____"

- "_____"

- "_____"

- "_____"

- "_____"

- "_____"

Classroom Situations—When helping teachers implement this trauma-informed model, here are some key tips to making this work successfully:

- Know which battles are worth taking on at that moment. If the student is becoming disruptive in class, coach the teacher to get the lesson going then quietly approach the student to check in and see what is going on.

"Ironically, consequences intended to create and motivate children often become the block that decreases or stifles motivation."

— *Heather T. Forbes, LCSW*

- Help teachers to understand that a student with his head down and not engaging is not disrupting the class. Use the same strategy—get the class lesson going and wait for the right moment to approach the student. When approaching the student, try to work toward a win/win situation, "I can tell this is not the best day for you, is there anything that I can help you with?"

- When a student is upset and isn't responding to the calming actions of the teacher, he may need to be removed from the classroom. Traditionally, this was done in a punitive and ousting manner, which only triggered a student's rejection and abandonment issues. Instead, offer the student a more productive alternative by saying something like, "I can see that you are really upset today. Would you prefer to take a break in ISS until you feel that you can get your stress level down?" Or, offer another option, "Would you like to speak to someone in the office?" Remember, if there is a relationship already built with the administration and the culture of connection has been established, the student knows he can go to the office to get help, not to be punished.

- If Billy responds that he is not going to "do any f---ing work," if possible, give him some more time to cool down and then quietly approach him again. "Wow! What brought that on?" Or, "What's going on...this doesn't sound like you?" Always be looking for options that will help the student de-escalate.

- Help teachers to understand that if you ask Billy to do a task he doesn't know how to do without support, it can dysregulate him. Fear of looking stupid in front of his peers will trigger him. If this happens, immediately step in with an alternative and shift the focus back onto you, "You know, Billy, as the teacher this is something I probably should do myself instead." Afterwards, away from the other students, process with Billy what happened and how his response was inappropriate and how he can develop better ways of expressing himself in the future.

- Help teachers to embrace negative situations. Some of the most intense situations can be the best relationship building opportunities when the teacher can follow the H4B Sequence. For instance, if Billy responds to the teacher personally with a "f--- you," the teacher can ask Billy (in a calm voice) to please step out in the hallway or walk over to where he is sitting. She can quietly ask, "Wow, what did

I say to bring that on?" The teacher can continue by saying, "You seem really upset. Would you like to put your head down on your desk until you are feeling better or would you like to take a break?" If Billy can positively respond, then the teacher can work through the entire H4B Sequence with Billy, without further assistance. However, if Billy escalates and continues to disrupt, he should be referred to the office.

Keep Yourself Regulated—Not only does working with students impacted by trauma require taking a new approach, it requires a tremendous amount of self-awareness. If you are not able to drop your personal mirror, it is super easy to become reactive. It must be kept in your awareness that Billy's behavior is not about you, rather, it's about Billy.

In *Help for Billy*, more in-depth information is given on how to keep regulated through the challenges of interacting with the toughest of our Billys who can be intensely dysregulated, disrespectful, and disobedient. It is strongly suggested that you read Chapter 9 in *Help for Billy* to find out more about how to stay regulated. These include the following:

- Relationship entrainment
- Nonverbal communication
- Cultural and personal beliefs
- Emotional awareness
- "Unfinished business"
- Window of stress tolerance

"During trauma, children learn 'self-care' in the absence of parental care. This can unfold into 'You aren't in charge of me' or 'I will never never trust you' or 'I'm in charge and you can't tell me what to do!' It is simply a fear of being vulnerable again."

— Heather T. Forbes, LCSW

Chapter 9 in *Help for Billy* also gives and explains in-depth several solutions for staying regulated such as:

- Validating yourself
- Taking care of yourself at school
- Taking care of yourself outside of school
- Understanding trauma
- Loving yourself

Dropping your personal mirror allows you to stay calm and seek the cause to the problem that is happening before you. When you are working with students who are escalated emotionally, if you stay calm, regulated, and emotionally connected, they will begin to feel safe.

The greatest change for Billy will be how you respond to him in the middle of one of his storms. When you respond to Billy in the "raw" moments, instead of reacting to him, change will happen. Progress will be seen over time as Billy can look at you for safety during the times he escalates, and thus, Billy will be on his journey to healing.

"Do not learn how to react. Learn how to respond."
– Buddha

CHAPTER SEVENTEEN

Classroom Strategies

In addition to helping students through your interactions, as described in the previous chapter, there are several strategies that can be put into place to support Billy in the classroom.

On the next three pages is a chart giving a comprehensive list of strategies to consider when implementing a trauma-informed school. The goals of using the strategies are grouped in the left-hand column in alphabetical order. The next two columns identify which strategies are recommended for elementary school and which ones are recommended for secondary schools. While some of the strategies may be recommended for both, the way they are implemented will need to be adjusted as needed to be age appropriate. On the pages that follow the chart, explanations of each strategy are given.

Please note that there is flexibility in this list. It should only be used as a guide. For instance, if your school is a secondary school but a majority of the students attending are developmentally delayed, some of the more juvenile strategies listed for elementary schools would be appropriate for you. Use your judgment and pick the strategies that will best fit the needs of your student population.

"When it comes to bad behavior, all roads lead back to fear, stress, and overwhelm."
– *Heather T. Forbes, LCSW*

STRATEGIES		
GOAL	ELEMENTARY STRATEGIES	SECONDARY STRATEGIES
BUILD RELATIONSHIP	• Leave a note on the student's desk • Have a struggling Billy come to the classroom before school • Lunch with the principal	• Connect with student during passing time • Assign mentor to Billys who need extra attention • Lunch with principal
BUILD SELF-ESTEEM	• Affirmations •Story Time	• Affirmations
CREATE A CALM CLASSROOM	• Warm lighting • Increase natural lighting if possible • Sound machine • Animals • Decrease wall hangings	• Warm lighting • Increase natural lighting if possible • Sound machine • Animals • Decrease wall hangings
CREATE A "FAMILY" IN THE CLASSROOM	• Pictures of each student on posterboard • Welcome each student by his/her name • Chart with "School Hierarchy"	• Welcome each student by his/her name • Chart with "School Hierarchy"
FOCUS ON BREATHING	• 2 min. meditation • Balloons • Bubbles • Pinwheels • Ring the Singing Bowl • Gonoodle.com	• 10-15 min. meditation • Ring the Singing Bowl • Gonoodle.com • Pinwheels
FOCUS ON SAFETY	•SafeZone in the classroom • Mantras	• SafeZone in the classroom • Mantras • In School Suspension Room

STRATEGIES CONTINUED		
GOAL	ELEMENTARY STRATEGIES	SECONDARY STRATEGIES
FOCUS ON REGULATION VS. DYSREGULATION	• Window of Stress Tolerance Worksheet • "Safe Keeper System" • Time-In • Before School • Anger Catcher • Calm Down Bottles • "Paint Chip" Plan • Picture • Phone call home • Coloring books • Listen to music • Stuffed Animals	• Teach Window of Stress Tolerance • Teach the Brain Science and the impact of trauma on the brain • Time-In • Knitting • Calm Down Bottles • "Paint Chip" Plan • Picture • Phone call or text home • Coloring Books • Listen to music
PROVIDE MOVEMENT OPPORTUNITIES	• Swinging • Rocking • Merry-go-round • Brain Gym ® exercises • Running • Gonoodle.com	• Taped Pacing Area • Rocking • "Walk, Talk, and Regulate" • Brain Gym ® exercises • Running [a] Gonoodle.com
PROVIDE PURPOSE	• Before School	• Before School
PROVIDE NOURISHMENT	• Have snacks and water available at all times	• Have snacks and water available at all times
PROVIDE STRUCTURE	• Be consistant • Keep Daily Schedule Visible • Create traditions	• Be consistant • Keep Daily Schedule Visible • Create traditions
SUPPORT TRANSITIONING	• Play soft music before the bell rings • Ringing the Singing Bowl to STOP	• Have staff present in the hallways during passing time • Ring the Singing Bowl to STOP
TEACH EMOTIONAL EXPRESSION	• Basic Feeling Words • Story Time	• Basic Feeling Words • Character Analysis

	STRATEGIES CONTINUED	
GOAL	ELEMENTARY STRATEGIES	SECONDARY STRATEGIES
TEACH HOW TO IDENTIFY STRESS	• *Stress Indicator Form* • Identify Visceral Reactions to Stress	• *Stress Indicator Form* • Identify Visceral Reactions to Stress
TEACH PROBLEM SOLVING SKILLS AND CRITICAL THINKING SKILLS	• *Liguisystems* • Character Analysis	• *Linguisystems* • Character Analysis
TEACH SOCIAL SKILLS	• *Linguisystems* • Group sessions with Guidance Counselor • Use Autism resources	• *Liguisystems* • Group sessions with the Guidance Couselor • Use Autism resources

1. Affirmations—One of the most challenging aspects of working with children impacted by trauma is that they believe they are unworthy, "losers," the "bad" kid, damaged, or worse. Helping them to build their self-esteem is critical to getting them to rekindle their innate love for learning and internal motivation. *Help for Billy* gives the specifics of ways to write effective affirmations (See Chapter 5 – Belief Systems in *Help for Billy*).

Be creative and see how you can incorporate affirmations in your core curriculum. Here are a few examples:

- Use affirmations for a spelling lesson.
- Ask students to identify characters in a story or novel that have negative belief systems and have them write affirmations that would help improve the character's belief systems. Subconsciously, students will identify their own negative belief systems in the characters.
- For elementary age students, put the affirmations to music and have the students sing them as part of your morning routine.

2. Anger Catcher—Turn the traditional "paper fortune teller" into an anger catcher to teach students how to deal with their stress and anger. Once the students create these, have them keep them at their desks to use when their stress levels increase as a reminder of what appropriate options they have.[1]

3. Animals—What is one commonality in the waiting room of every counseling office? Easy...a fish tank. Animals are a wonderful way to help students regulate. Bunnies, hamsters, guinea pigs, and as mentioned, fish, can be used to calm dysregulated students. Some schools are using therapy dogs in the classroom to help regulate students. This strategy does take the commitment of teachers to care for the animals all year long.

4. Autism Resources—Some of the main characteristics of a child diagnosed with autism are strikingly similar to a student impacted by trauma. These include deficits in social skills, language development, emotional expressive skills, sensory issues, and transitional struggles. Here are a few examples of typical characteristics of children with autism that parallel Billy's challenges:

- Difficulty initiating social interactions
- Minimal acknowledgment of others
- Unable to understand other people's feelings
- Difficulty reading facial expressions and body language correctly.
- Often uses short, incomplete sentences
- Obsessions with objects, ideas, or desires
- Perfectionism in certain areas.
- Transitioning from one activity to another is difficult
- Verbal outbursts
- Difficulty sensing time
- Difficulty with loud or sudden sounds
- Resists change in the environment
- Becomes overwhelmed with too much verbal direction
- Difficulty with reading comprehension
- Short attention span for most lessons
- Resistance or inability to following directions

This list should look very familiar to the Billys of your school. While Billy may not actually be autistic, the point is that the resources available for children with autism are fantastic for helping our students impacted by trauma. Check with your district's special education resource specialist for autism related resources the district may already have available for use.

5. Balloons—Balloons are a fantastic way to get students to start breathing, even our older students. Since air is invisible, the concept of breathing is a bit nebulous. Blowing into a balloon makes breathing more tangible and concrete.

Balloons can also be a way to help students release their anger. Have Billy blow-up a red balloon (symbolizing anger). Don't tie it up; simply pinch the end. Have Billy draw a face to represent his feelings on the balloon. Before Billy releases the balloon, help him to imagine all his feelings being released with the balloon and have him take a deep breathe before releasing the balloon.

6. Before School—As the old adage goes, "An ounce of prevention is worth a pound of cure," getting Billy regulated at the beginning of the school day can help to divert major blowouts the rest of the day. Have Billy come to his teacher's room when he gets off the bus instead of going to the courtyard with all the other students before school. For secondary schools, have him go to either his homeroom teacher or the teacher to whom he is most connected. He can be given a job each morning like cleaning off the white board, sharpening pencils, or passing out papers. Giving Billy a job to do gives him purpose. It also makes him feel needed and an important part of how the classroom functions.

Spending this time in the morning in the classroom can also be an important time to strengthen Billy's relationship with his teacher. This does require the teacher being available these last ten minutes before school starts which can be a critical time in the morning for a teacher. However, this investment in time to connect with Billy can save time later in the classroom. It will take proactive thinking but the payoff can be tremendous.

7. Brain Gym®—The Brain Gym® activities recall the movements naturally done by a child during the first years of life when a child is learning to coordinate his eyes, ears, hands, and whole body. The movements, exercises, and activities help to improve a student's ability to listen, comprehend, concentrate, and focus. These movements have also been shown to improve memory, organizational skills, and academic learning by connecting the left and right hemispheres. The activities are simple yet truly effective.

These movements can be incorporated while teaching a lesson. For instance, one classroom teacher had her students stand up during math to learn to count by two's. As she led them through counting by two's, she also had them do the cross crawl. The cross crawl is done in a standing position and lifting one leg while tapping the knee of this leg to the hand of the opposite arm. Then, repeating this body pattern, alternating left and right sides while simultaneously counting by two's the students were learning while adding movement to their learning.

Visit the Brain Gym® website at: www.braingym.org for more information and training opportunities.

8. Bubbles—Getting students to do some deep breathing can be boring and uninteresting to them. You can't see air, so it doesn't seem purposeful to them, or fun for that matter. However, getting children to blow bubbles is fun and takes very little effort to get them initiated in such an activity. Blowing bubbles can be an activity you do as an entire class (when you're outside) as a proactive way to keeping students regulated, or it can be done on an individual basis when Billy might need a break from the classroom when he is beginning to get dysregulated.

"If you know the art of breathing you have the strength, wisdom, and courage of ten tigers."
– *Chinese Adage*

9. Calm Down Bottles—Sometimes students are too overwhelmed to be able to engage in a regulatory activity with an adult, one-on-one. Adult interactions can challenge their nervous systems because adult interactions in their history weren't always safe. Giving students a regulatory activity they can do on their own may be the best option. "Calm Down Bottles" can be an excellent tool to help settle their nervous systems.

Have a dysregulated student shake the bottle as hard as he wants to (do not make them out of glass—plastic only). The shaking provides input into the body, which helps to release some of the energy and gives a less destructive outlet than kicking or hitting. The student then holds the bottle still and watches the glitter fall. This centers the student's hands and eyes and helps to organize and align his nervous system. The slow fall of the shaken glitter is a visual representation of slowing the heart rate and breathing.

10. Character Analysis—It can be much easier to see ways to help other people improve themselves than it can be to look in a mirror and see where we ourselves need improvement. Have students do a character analysis, of sorts, on a character in a book you read (for younger students) or in a novel they read (for older students) by describing the regulation or dysregulation of the character. Have them identify how the character acts when he/she is dysregulated, what are the triggers that dysregulate the character, and what coping skills the character uses to get re-regulated (both positive and negative coping skills). You can also teach emotional expression with this exercise and ask the student to describe how the character is feeling in certain scenes. This is a wonderful way to accomplish the required reading of the curriculum while simultaneously teaching students emotional intelligence.

11. Coloring Books—Coloring books aren't just for young children. They offer several therapeutic benefits for older children and even adults. Coloring books with repetitive patterns can help to calm the brain and help the user reach an almost meditative state. They can help to de-stress and reduce anxiety. Best of all, there are several websites where you can download pages for free. Offer a five or ten minute break to Billy when he gets dysregulated to be able to color. This time away from academics will help him calm his brain to get re-centered and back to his academics recharged and balanced.

12. Consistency—We've always known that consistency is important for children but for children impacted by trauma, consistency becomes even more critical. This is because one of the characteristics of trauma is that it happens by surprise. Children impacted by trauma begin to believe that when change happens, pain happens...it is their blueprint for living. Having a consistent environment creates a tremendous amount of safety because they know what will happen next and what to expect. They don't have to spend their time and energy wondering and worrying about what will happen and what will come next. They can stay in the present moment and begin to learn to relax. Thus, keeping rules and expectations the same from moment to moment is vitally important to creating an environment of safety for our Billys.

13. Daily Schedules—Along the same vein as "Consistency," is the necessity of posting daily schedules for students. It might seem unnecessary after a few weeks of school because the schedule is the same and you feel as if the students know exactly what will happen next. Billy, however, is a concrete thinker. In his mind, if it isn't written down, then it isn't going to happen. It might be the 100th day of school and for the past 100 days, you've had the same schedule. However, even for the next 100 days of school, it will be necessary to keep writing down the schedule. It gives Billy the safety and security he needs so he knows with more certainty what is going to happen next. It is a very effective tool to help calm anxiety.

14. "Family" Pictures—We are biologically designed to be in community. Dr. Bruce Lipton, a world-renowned developmental and cellular biologist, states, "human beings are not meant to be alone. There is a fundamental biological imperative that propels you and every organism on this planet to be in a community, to be in relationship with other organisms." (Bruce H. Lipton, The Honeymoon Effect: The Science of Creating Heaven on Earth). Our Andys come to school with a sense of belonging. They have a strong family structure that gives them a knowing that they are special and an important part of a greater whole. Billy does not. He doesn't know he is important. He doesn't know he is special. He doesn't know he belongs. He does believe he is alone.

For Billy, school becomes his family. He needs his school family to give him what Andy has at home. To do this, create a poster or bulletin board that visually shows the class "family." Showcase the family with pictures of each student and talk about how the class is a family in your lessons and conversations. While we may consider this to be something we only do for elementary school students, it is as needed for our secondary students. The approach to your design of the bulletin board should be less juvenile but certainly should convey the same message: this class is your family and you are an important part of who we are as a whole.

We all need to belong, whether we are six or sixteen, or even sixty-six.

15. Feeling Sticks—This strategy is effective and a very quick check that allows the teacher to be aware of the students' emotional state each morning when each student comes into the classroom. Have a spot in which you can set up the strategy, close to the door, so students follow the routine of identifying their feelings each morning.

On a table or counter, have large Popsicle sticks or tongue depressors and write each student's name on his/her own stick. Next to the Popsicle sticks, have a greeting that asks, "How are you feeling this morning?" Make five containers for the students to place their Popsicle into that are marked as follows: 1) "I'm happy, 2) "I'm scared," 3) "I'm sad," 4) "I'm mad," and 5) "I'm grateful."

During the first hour of the morning, have each Billy place his stick in the container that best describes how he is feeling that day. The teacher then immediately knows the emotional state of each of her students. The teacher makes a mental note and makes sure she checks in with each Billy who puts his feeling stick in the mad, sad, or scared cups and asks if there is anything they can do to help the student feel better. She might make some suggestions to Billy or simply listen to what is going on in Billy's life. Whether it is that he hasn't eaten breakfast or his brother was being mean to him, acknowledging Billy's frustration at the beginning of the day helps Billy regulate and start the day on a positive note.

16. Feeling Words—Many times, we work to teach feelings to students and we overwhelm them in the process because we give them too many words. Make it simple...there are five basic feeling words that students need to be taught:

1) Mad

2) Happy

3) Scared

4) Sad

5) Grateful

MAD   HAPPY   SCARED   SAD   GRATEFUL

© Joanna Forbes, 2016 [2]

17. GoNoodle.com—GoNoodle.com was launched in 2013 and it is a free resource for schools to help students improve their self-regulatory skills and channel their physical and emotional energy. The GoNoodle.com website offers short movement videos (three-to-five minutes in length) that allow teachers to engage students in movement with dancing, stretching, running, and mindfulness activities. Use their videos and activities throughout the day to give your students a "brain break." Not only will these videos help students improve their behavior, it will help them improve their focus and help them engage better academically.

18. Humor—One of the most powerful coping mechanisms we have available to us is humor. Humor strengthens relationships and it calms down our nervous system. Research even suggests that humor improves your immune system. However, this coping mechanism seems to be the least available when we need it the most—when times are stressful. Make it a point to find the humor in whatever happens, good or bad with Billy. Help Billy find the humor in situations so he can learn to lighten his mood and free up his energy to problem-solve and build connection.

19. In School Suspension—Please see Chapter 8 for the complete explanation of In School Suspensions.

20. Knitting—Knitting isn't just for your grandmother. Neuroscience is showing that doing repetitive, rhythmic, and patterned activities calm the brain. Knitting can lower the heart rate and reduce the stress hormone, cortisol, in the body. Knitting is something students can do with their hands while still listening attentively in class. It is also an activity students can participate in when they go to the Calm Room or In School Suspension Room to take a ten-minute break. Have students come into school before the school bell rings instead of the courtyard in the morning. Create a knitting circle for students to join and have them knit caps for newborns and baby blankets for the local hospital's neonatal unit. This type of activity would get the students connected socially, give them a sense of purpose, and regulate them to begin the school day.[3]

Other crafting activities such as crocheting can have the same benefit as knitting.

21. Lighting—As humans, we are designed to live in unfiltered sunlight with the full spectrum of lighting. Fluorescent lighting, however, typically only offers one color spectrum. Fluorescent lighting also emits "flicker," which has been shown to trigger nervous system issues and a loss of energy in sensitive individuals. Due to Billy's trauma, his nervous system is very sensitive, and it needs to be considered that fluorescent lighting can be increasing his level of dysregulation.

If natural lighting is possible, pull up the shades and allow full spectrum lighting into your classrooms as much as possible. Add some lamps with incandescent bulbs, as well. Replace some of your plain plastic fluorescent panels with "sky panels" or any other type of fluorescent light diffuser panels to help reduce the harsh glare that can emanate from the fluorescent lighting.

And while you're at it, add a few plants and greenery to give more warmth and life to your classrooms.

22. Linguisystems—One of the best ways to teach students problem solving skills, critical thinking skills, and social interaction skills is through the resources available from www.linguisystems.com. Linguisystems has a wide variety of resources that range in all different grade levels. Due to Billy's lack of ability to interact socially and his tendency to think in concrete terms, it can be very helpful to use some of the resources designed for students diagnosed with autism. Also, look for any of their resources that address "social language development" skills. Below are a few examples:

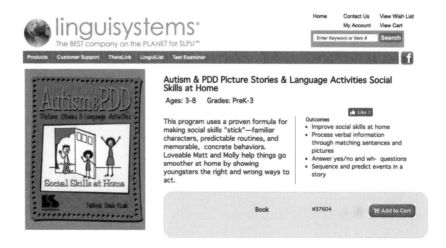

23. Lunch with the Principal—Traditionally, students have viewed the principal as an authoritative figure to be feared. For Andy, this has worked to keep him inside the boundaries and following the rules. For Billy, however, fear only makes him more dysregulated and more prone to act out. Having Billy build a strong relationship with the principal is much more effective. For your most challenging Billys, set a time to meet with him to have lunch and get to know him better. Food is one of the best ways to calm someone and connect with him/her. The conversation should center around what is going on in Billy's life, not how he should behave better or what rules he needs to follow It is simply a time to connect and build relationship. Being a "Mister Rogers" during a lunch connection will give you the ability to more effectively be a "General Patton" when needed in the future.

24. Mantras—For our Billys in the classroom who have a tendency to be unsafe, the use of mantras can be an effective way to stop them from crossing the line of safety. Mantras help students stay connected with the teacher and they offer a simple, repetitive, and familiar dialogue to keep students from slipping down into the lower parts of the brain. If Billy begins to become deeply dysregulated, his ability to process language is severely compromised. If the teacher were to talk to him in sentences like, "Billy, you need to stop that now because you're becoming unsafe and that's not good for any of us. Put that down right now, Billy. You need to sit down and take a deep breath and calm down.", Billy would become even more dysregulated. Long complex dialogue sounds more to Billy like the teacher on the Peanuts cartoon, "Wah wah wah wah wah wah wah wah wah wah...." It irritates him and can shift him further down into the midbrain or even the reptilian brain.

Instead, use mantras at the start of each day and repeat them as a class throughout the day a couple more times. Post the mantras with high visibility. The visual of the mantras helps to reinforce the memorization of the mantras. Billy's auditory processing is typically much weaker than his visual processing.

The mantras go like this:

> Teacher: "Who's safe at (insert school name)?"
>
> Students: "I am safe!"
>
> Teacher: "All of the time or some of the time?"
>
> Students: "All of the time!"
>
> Teacher: "Who is in charge to keep you safe?"
>
> Students: "You, the teachers keep me safe!"
>
> Teacher: "All of the time!"

When the teacher sees Billy starting to decompensate and slip into a state of dysregulation, she can immediately go to the above dialogue instead of sounding like the Peanuts teacher. Because the mantras are familiar and simple, it can be just enough language to pull him up into his neocortex where he can think more rationally. The use of mantras has been used effectively in both elementary and secondary schools.

25. Meditation—Schools focusing on mindfulness are incorporating meditation into their daily schedules. Students report that they feel so much better after meditating for 10 to 15 minutes. Even students diagnosed with anxiety disorders report being less anxious afterwards. Principals are reporting that the climate of the school is much better after implementing mindfulness activities such as meditation.

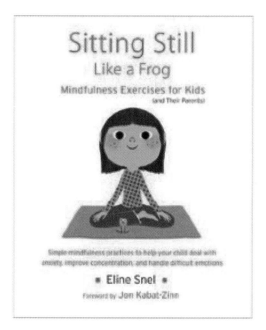

Meditation is easily learned and can be done while sitting comfortably at a desk with the eyes closed (or even open for Billy who might have too much fear to close his eyes). It doesn't require a yoga mat or anything extra. Add a time for meditation for students who need to settle their nervous systems or for entire classrooms before the school day begins.

A good book that includes a CD for younger students is "Sitting Like a Frog" by Eline Snel and Jon Kabat-Zinn.

Other resources for older students are available on the internet at:

1. The David Lynch Foundation
   www.davidlynchfoundation.org/schools.html.
2. "How to Start a Meditation Program in Your School
   www.edutopia.org/stw-student-stress-meditation-school-tips

26. Mentors—Some of our Billys may need more one-on-one support. Connecting them with a mentor can be an excellent way to get them more secure in their place in this world. It has been shown that students with mentors improve their attitude about school, increase their self-esteem and self-confidence, make better lifestyle choices, and have better high school graduation rates. Expand your thinking about who could serve as a mentor for some of your students. Perhaps it is someone already employed by your school district—a maintenance person, janitor, bus driver, or a cafeteria worker. Extending your reach into the community might also be an option—Boys and Girls Club, the faith community, or a community senior center.

Posted in: BuzzWorthy   Posted: June 6, 2015

Elementary School Students Line Up To Get Yearbooks Signed By Custodian, Photo Goes Viral

At one school in Illinois, the janitor was one of the most favored staff at the entire school. "Mr. Steve" was the one the students went to when they needed support because they knew that if anything were to happen, Mr. Steve was going to take care of it. Students lined up and patiently waited to get his autograph in their yearbooks because he had built a special bond with the students at the elementary school.

27. **Merry-Go-Round.** For students with any level of sensory processing issues and for many of our students with autism, a spin on the school merry-go-round (or few minutes on a "Sit n Spin) may be exactly what they need to get themselves regulated again. Spinning provides vestibular input to the body and many of our Billys crave this type of activity. The spinning can help to reorganize their neurological systems, giving them a greater ability to focus and be calm. For the students who need this, create a few "Spinning" passes that they can use during the day when they begin to feel dysregulated.

One student who needed vestibular input found the elevator to be his "tool" for getting regulated. He kept running out of the classroom to ride the elevator. When looking closer at this "negative" behavior, it became obvious that he was giving his teachers the solution to what he needed to calm down. Instead of him running out of the classroom without asking, he was then given "elevator" passes to cash-in throughout the day when needed. This way, he wasn't breaking the rules any more but he was also getting the vestibular input he was craving.

28. Music—Music (especially music without lyrics) is processed on the right side of the brain, which is the access point down into the limbic system. It has the power to calm this part of the brain and can help Billy move from a bottom-up control to a top-down control. It has been discovered that half an hour of classical music or other soothing melodies produces the same effect as 10mg of Valium. The following are genres of music than are effective at relaxing the brain, although music is subjective so it will also depend on the individual:

- Native American
- Celtic
- Instrumental
- Acoustic
- Classical
- Smooth Jazz
- Drumming
- Soul
- Lullabies
- Piano music
- Sound of nature (thunder, rain, waves, etc.), especially when

mixed with other music such as light jazz, classical and easy listening.

29. Paint Chip Plan—When Billy begins to get dysregulated, it can be very difficult to access his memory...all the blood flow is going to his emotional brain, not his thinking brain. Remembering what to do when he gets into a negative emotional state is almost impossible for him when he hasn't had enough practice to make it a habit. Help Billy (or the entire class) create a "paint chip plan." On a paint chip (that can be picked up for free from a building supply store), write down the different coping skills that Billy has identified as helpful to him. It is important not to tell him what to write on the plan...it has to be his idea to work. Many of the strategies listed in this chapter can be suggested to Billy along with the following:

- Talk it out

- Ask for a break

- Ask for a time-out in the safe room or ISS

- Take three deep breaths

- Meet with his mentor

- Check-in with his body

Have Billy carry this in his pocket or at the elementary school level, have students tape it to the top of their desks.

30. Passing Time—When students are in the hallways, having a strong staff presence is ideal. Passing time is an excellent time for teachers to be standing at their doors connecting with students, welcoming them into their classes, and monitoring what is going on in the hallway. Encourage teachers to use this time for relationship building instead of lesson planning or other things. Please see Chapter 10 for more information on this.

31. Phone Call Home—As adults, very few of us go through an entire workday without checking in with our spouse, partner, or significant other. We call. We text. We email. We find ways to connect with them as a way to remain connected and calm during a stressful day at work. Our students, however, are expected to go through an entire school day with no connection. This is especially true for our younger students who don't have cellphones and it is these students who are most fragile in their need for parental connection.

Some of our Billys aren't neurologically or developmentally ready to be in the school environment for a full day without their parents. If Billy has a strong relationship with his parent(s), make it part of his daily schedule to be able to call his parent to connect. This should take less than two minutes but in these two minutes, Billy has the ability to get regulated enough to successfully make it through the rest of the day. The conversation can be as simple as:

> Billy: "Hi, Mom."
>
> Mom: "Hi, Billy! How's it going?"
>
> Billy: "It's okay."
>
> Mom: "I know it's hard work being in school and working so hard. I miss you, Billy."
>
> Billy: "I miss you, too."
>
> Mom: "I'll be there at 3:30 to pick you up. I can't wait to see you then. Have a good afternoon, sweetheart."
>
> Billy: "Okay."
>
> Mom: "I love you. See you soon."
>
> Billy: "Bye."

Having a phone call home may not be possible with every student, nor is it needed for every student. But for some of your Billys, it is just what they need to increase their window of stress tolerance.

32. Picture—Many of our Billys may have histories of abandonment and loss, such as the Billys in your school who were adopted. It is typical of many of these students to fear losing their parents, again. Due to the lag in Billy's developmental process and because of his concrete thinking, being at school can be exceptionally stressful. When he is away from his family, he has a hard time understanding that his family is still there for him. Carrying around a picture in his backpack or pocket can be a way for him to quickly pull out the picture to remind him that he is okay. Having a visual reminder can be much more impactful than simply saying to Billy, "You're okay, Billy. Your mom/dad will be here later to get you."

And if we think about it, most of us as grown adults, have pictures of our family on our desks at work, as well.

33. Pinwheels—Pinwheels offer a visual outcome of breathing. Have students practice breathing deeply by breathing in and then exhaling to control the speed of the pinwheel. It will give them a sense of control and help them change their focus from what is triggering them to creating beauty with the pinwheel.

34. Rocking—Rocking isn't just for our preschoolers anymore. In fact, the 35th president of the United States, John F. Kennedy, was famous for having a rocking chair at the White House, and even on Air Force One for his chronic back pain.[1]

Research is showing that rocking, with it's rhythmic motion, calms the brain and soothes the nervous system. Some teachers have reported that the use of a rocker for their students with ADD or ADHD has increased these students ability to focus because rocking satisfies the need to keep moving. Keep a rocking chair in the classroom, safe room, or ISS to give students the option of rocking to calm down and get regulated.

35. Running—Physical exercise is one of the top three ways of regulating the body (oxygen and food being the other two). Taking five minutes to run around the track or around the school campus might be exactly what Billy needs to get settled back down enough to focus in class and engage in his academics.

36. Safe Keeper System—*The Safe Keeper System* is based on teaching children life skills and provides the student with new chances in every moment to self-correct and re-regulate. Two teachers, Sally Haughey and Mary Myers, developed it.[3]

This system is based on the idea that children are learning and want to make the right choices; they just need a little support and regulatory help to get there. This approach is based on the following beliefs:

- Children have a need to be safe.
- Children have a need to be taught how to regulate in order to behave.
- Learning is a process.
- Practice, not punishment, teaches a child how to behave through modeling and good role models.
- Mutual respect and honor are the motivators of compliance.

The *Safe Keeper System* takes the place of the *Red Light Classroom Management* plan. The color card system of green, yellow, and red works to control children by giving punishments for consequences. There is never a chance for a child to correct his/her behavior that day. They can't return to the green until the next day. This is in contrast to the Safe Keeper System that allows students to correct their behavior in the now, within the support of a safe relationship.

The *Safe Keeper System* works with the concept of how a mother Kangaroo keeps her baby safe in her pouch. Each Billy can design his pouch in any way he chooses. Billy places his kangaroo (with his name written on the Popsicle stick) in his pouch. This is Billy's safe spot. The teacher's pouch, the Safe Pocket, is at the top of the mountain on the brown background.

When a student begins to get dysregulated, the teacher can place that student's kangaroo in her Safe Pocket at the top. This brings awareness to both the student and teacher that the student may need some help getting regulated. Some typical examples of behaviors that will demonstrate a student's regulatory state are as follows:

- Billy has needed extra reminders to follow directions.

- Billy is not being kind, showing respect, or being helpful.

- Billy is struggling to get his work done when prompted.

This is a regulatory-based system that identifies "misbehavior" as a regulation issue, not a behavior issue. By putting the student's kangaroo in the teacher's pouch, it simply says that the student has shifted from a state of regulation to a state of dysregulation. It gives the student the opportunity to learn how to regulate and how to handle stress better.

Some teachers have even reported that when a student was feeling dysregulated, instead of acting out, they simply went up to the Safe Keeper System and put their kangaroo inside the teacher's pocket themselves. That gave the teacher the signal that the student needed to connect and relate and it saved the teacher from having to deal with any negative behaviors from the student. This system holds the student accountable in a safe environment and without punitive consequences and it helps to build strong relationships.

The *Safe Keeper System* is an effective strategy for behavior management first because it is a regulatory-based system and second, it is built around kindness and safety. There are five points to a star, and there are five expected behaviors for the classroom.

1. Be Respectful – I treat others how I want to be treated Are you being polite or rude?

2. Be Responsible – I do the right thing and can be trusted to do what needs to be done. Are you being trustworthy or careless?

3. Be Patient – I can wait calmly for someone or something. Are you being calm or restless?

4. Be Careful – I treat friends and things in a gentle way. Are you being gentle or rough?

5. Be Helpful – My words and actions help not hurt others. Are you being helpful or hurtful?

This system has to be taught before implementation. It is very important to process with the students how the system works and it should always be guided in a calm and respectful environment.

37. Safe Zone—The *Safe Zone* is a designated area inside the classroom for students to go when they get overwhelmed and need a quick break. The *Safe Zone* is a safe place for students to feel their emotions and process what has triggered them into a fear state. All classrooms in the school should have a *Safe Zone*.

The ideal spot to set up a *Safe Zone* is behind the teacher's desk. This provides the student with a safe place away from the other students and near the teacher. As the teacher builds a caring adult relationship with the Billys of the classroom, they will grow to understand that they can look to the teacher for safety and security.

The teacher should teach the students the following concepts about the *Safe Zone*:

- The teacher is the safest person in the classroom and students are encouraged to come to the teacher when they aren't feeling safe. Taking a few moments in the *Safe Zone* with the help of their teacher may be just what they need to get back on task.

- It is a place for them to go if they are feeling sad, mad, or scared. It is a place for them to take the time they need to cool down and talk about what is bothering them. They don't have to ask to go to the *Safe Zone*. It is open for them

- Only one student at a time is allowed to be in the *Safe Zone*. If a student needs the *Safe Zone* and there is already a student there, they need to let the teacher know they need a time, as well, in the *Safe Zone*.

- Students cannot stay in the *Safe Zone* all day. If the teacher determines they have spent their allotted time in the *Safe Zone* but they aren't ready to go back to their desk, they are welcome at that point to go to the *Calm Room* to get more help.

- If a student is upset and the teacher asks the student to go to the *Safe Zone*, the student is NOT in trouble. The teacher is only asking the student to go to the *Safe Zone* so they have a place to calm down and feel safe. The student will be welcomed back to rejoin the class when they are regulated. There are no consequences for going to the *Safe Zone*.

- The *Safe Zone* is not a punitive "Time-out." It is completely the opposite...it is a place open to every student to take a break so they don't do something they don't want to do. It is a place to refocus so they can make the right decisions and stay within the boundaries.

The *Safe Zone* is different from the *Calm Room* because it is located inside the classroom. The *Safe Zone* is designed to keep Billy in the classroom so he remains part of the "classroom family" even when he is upset. It is the first tier of intervention. For times that Billy needs more one-on-one intervention and more intense help calming down, he would then go to the *Calm Room*.

38. School Hierarchy Poster—Babies come into this world expecting adults to take care of them and to protect them. When this system fails, as in Billy's case, they develop a belief system that all adults are unsafe and thus, the only option is to be in charge of themselves. They refuse to allow anyone to be in charge of them because they don't want to get hurt again. Feeling vulnerability at such a young age shifts their entire perspective and this is what causes power struggles in the classroom. When Billy walks into Kindergarten and says to his teacher "You're not in charge of me; I am!" work has to be done to re-establish hierarchy in the classroom.

Drawing a hierarchy poster to illustrate to your students the hierarchy of the school can be an effective visual. In large corporations, there is typically an organizational chart to show the corporate structure. It makes it clear to the employees to whom they are to report. The same is needed in the classroom with Billy because he doesn't have a blueprint of family structure. In fact, some of our Billys are coming from homes where they are not only the parents to their siblings; they are also taking care of their own parents. The idea of having someone in charge of them is a foreign concept and unfortunately, we have always recognized this in negative terms by saying that Billy "has problems with authority." The solution is to teach him about hierarchy in a functioning system such as the school environment. This will not only help him in school, it will give him a solid working blueprint of how organizations work when he enters the work force.

When presenting this hierarchy chart to the class, it is important to stress that the people in charge of the students (the teacher, vice-principal, principal, SRO) are in charge to keep the students safe and to make sure they have their needs met at school. It needs to be stressed that these authority figures are not in charge to simply have power over them but to take care of them, guide them, and help them.

Words that define the school culture can be added to the chart, as well. You have to redefine what a functional environment means to Billy. Words to define this new world to Billy can include the following: safety, security, inclusive, unconditional, acceptance, safe base, stability, endurance, fun, joy, respect, hierarchy, and love.

This hierarchy chart needs to be reviewed every day at the beginning of the school year and kept in the classroom as a visual reminder.

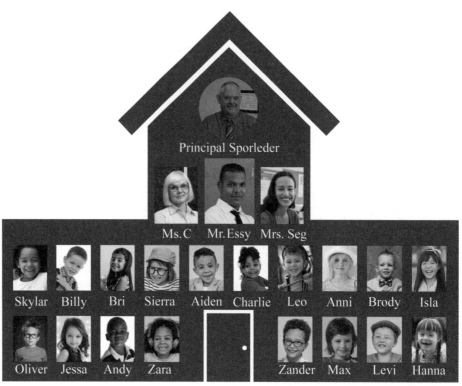

OUR CLASS IS A FAMILY

39. Sing—Singing together as a classroom builds community and enhances resilience. When most of us grew up, we would sing patriotic songs after saying the pledge of allegiance. Singing together was a way to also strengthen the bond of the entire classroom. Unfortunately, this singing has gone by the wayside. It's time to bring it back to help our students regulate and connect, again. The internet, especially YouTube, is full of ideas of songs that can be used for children or you can be creative and create your own songs that teach about regulation, calming down, and connecting with one another. Additionally, songs that teach academics such as spelling and arithmetic should also be included (YouTube is filled with videos from The Ron Clark Academy that are inspiring.)

40. Singing Bowl—There will be times in the classroom where the energy begins to build and the students are beginning to get dysregulated. Stopping this negative momentum will be key in keeping the class cohesive and regulated. Use a "singing bowl" to stop everything at that moment and lead the class in a couple of deep breaths. The ringing of the singing bowl is soothing and when used consistently, the students begin to automatically recognize it as a time to breathe and re-regulated.

The singing bowl can also be used when you start the class for the day, leading the class in 30 seconds of breathing before any academics begins. It is not only good for the students, it helps the teacher also get centered and balanced before starting the lesson.

Singing bowls can easily be purchased off the internet by googling "singing bowl." There are several apps available for smart phones for free or at a small charge that create the sound of singing bowls.

41. Snacks and Water—Hunger and thirst are on the bottom of the "Hierarchy of Learning" pyramid discussed in Chapter 4. Keeping small snacks and water available for the students in the classroom can be a very effective strategy to keeping students regulated. Maintaining a child's blood sugar level can do wonders for keeping them focused and keeping their behaviors in line.

Be sure to watch the sugar content on the snacks you provide. Many snacks will promote themselves as healthy snacks but in reality, they are overly processed and contain a huge amount of sugar. Raisins, granola bars, apples, and nuts are good choices.

42. Social Skills Groups—Most of our Billys need additional support to build better social skills. Their blueprint for relationships is skewed and they typically have deep fears of being rejected, which hinder their ability to form healthy and enjoyable relationships. Social skills deficits aren't only troubling our younger students; they are prevalent in our older students, especially when they enter into intimate dating relationships.

Social skills groups can help students learn and practice important life skills such as the art of conversation and reading nonverbal communication. These groups can also teach how to respectfully respond to others, how to ask for help, and how to share and take turns.

While some attention can be given to this in the classroom, having a psychologist, social worker, guidance counselor, or therapist to provide social skills groups in your school may be what is needed for your Billys.

43. Sound Machine—Sound machines emit a consistent, soothing sound of rushing air. They can help to block out noises outside of the classroom, giving your students, especially Billy who is hypervigilent, a greater ability to concentrate and focus on what is in front of them, rather than what is going on outside the classroom. They also help Billy feel safer when his body isn't reacting to every noise being heard outside of the classroom. A cheaper solution is to use a box fan as that will also create a consistent, low-level noise and you might already have one on hand.

44. Story Time—Story time is an excellent opportunity to teach emotional intelligence. During the story and after the story, ask the students how the characters felt. It is easiest to choose books that are already geared towards teaching emotional expression, but teachers can be creative and turn almost any book into an emotional teaching tool. Here are a few suggested titles:

• "The Color Monster: A Pop-Up Book of Feelings"
  by Anna Llenas

- "Today I Feel Silly & Other Moods" by Jamie Lee Curtis

- "When I Feel Angry" by Cornelia Maude Spelman

- "Don't Need Friends" by Carolyn Crimi

Additionally, story time can be an opportunity to help build self-esteem and self-awareness. Here are two suggested titles:

- "I'm Gonna Like Me: Letting Off a Little Self-Esteem"
  by Jamie Lee Curtis

- "I Think, I Am!" by Louise Hay and Kristina Tracy

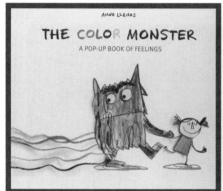  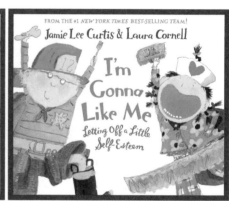

45. Stress Indicator Form—Please see Chapter 15 and the Appendix for the more information on the *Stress Indicator Form*.

46. Stuffed Animals—Stuffed animals are a universal symbol of comfort. They are soft, cuddly, and always smiling. We often associate stuffed animals with toddlers and preschoolers, but research is showing that they can be a great source of comfort for people with depression and anxiety. A study out of the University of Amsterdam found that snuggling a teddy bear was just as effective in providing comfort and reducing levels of anxiety around thoughts of death as having human-to-human contact.[4]

While it may not be appropriate to offer a stuffed animal to a middle or high school student in the classroom due to social pressure and judgment from peers, it might be something to consider for the guidance counselor or on-campus therapist when doing one-on-one work with your older students. But certainly for our younger students, having stuffed animals to hold while working on an assignment might be the perfect solution to calm them down enough to focus on their academics.

47. Swinging—There are tremendous neurological benefits to swinging on a swing set. The soothing and repetitive motion of a swing helps to calm, balance, and settle the brain. Swinging also offers vestibular input to the physical body, helping students with any sensory processing issues. When a student gets dysregulated and needs a break, offer a 5-minute swinging break before going back into the classroom.

48. Time-In—"Time-out" is familiar to all of us and has traditionally been used as a consequence for children who exhibit negative behavior. It, however, is a punitive response to a child and it also isolates them from everyone. Punishment without relationship only works to heighten Billy's stress level, so time-out is definitely one of the worst types of strategies we could ever use on him.

Instead, use a "Time-In" with Billy. Instead of being sent to time-out, the student is invited for a time-in with the teacher (or other staff member). The teacher helps Billy feel better and shift from a state of dysregulation to a state of regulation. Sometimes, when the teacher is too busy giving a lesson to have individual time with Billy, Billy can simply sit next to the teacher while she finishes up the lesson and instructions to the rest of the class. Having Billy sitting next to a regulated teacher can be enough to help him stop the negative behavior and get reconnected. Once the teacher is finished with the whole class, she can then check-in with Billy and see if he needs more time-in or if he is ready to go back to his desk.

If the concept of time-in seems like it rewards bad behavior by giving the child attention, it will take going back to the core concept we know about our Billys...their negative behaviors stem from a state of dysregulation. It is a regulatory issue, not a behavioral issue. Time-in allows Billy a chance, within the context of a safe adult relationship, to move back to a state of regulation. Billy can't just make a better choice to behave; he needs the assistance of a strong regulatory figure to calm his brain so he can then get back to making the right choices from a regulated state.

49. Traditions—Traditions are an important part of our families and thus, should be an important part of Billy's school family. Traditions offer predictability and certainty because Billy knows what to expect. Trauma happens by surprise so offering activities that are the opposite of surprise (traditions), creates a safe world for Billy. Traditions also create a sense of identity for the school and create a sense of pride for those who engage in the traditions.

Think of ways to create weekly traditions such as Pizza Wednesday or Spirit Friday where students wear the school colors. When one Billy was asked what would make school better, his response was, "Keep things the same on the same days." Our Billys crave structure and predictability.

50. Visceral Reactions—When we become stressed-out or experience negative emotions like anger, frustration, or sadness, the first place these reactions show up is in our physical bodies. Before conscious thought, we experience involuntary physical reactions such as heart pounding, adrenaline surging, racing pulse, stomach clenching, chest tightening, throat tightening, or face flushing. These reactions are immediate and always experienced first. One way to be one step ahead of reacting in a negative behavioral way to a stressful event is to become mindful of these visceral reactions...they are our "friends" because they give us a warning that we have become dysregulated.

We want to help our students, both the Billys and the Andys of the classroom, to become aware of their visceral reactions. Help students by asking them in the moment, "Where in your body do you feel your anger?" Have them breathe through the bodily response, connecting their mind and body together—connecting the thought with the visceral response.

It isn't a matter of making the visceral response "go away," but rather a matter of letting it pass and acknowledging the emotional response that goes along with it. Instead of projecting the emotional response through yelling, screaming, hitting, or the like, the student can learn to sit with the reaction, own it, and take control over it by breathing and acknowledging the feeling instead of letting it take control of the student. This takes practice and it is something that even the adults in the school should practice and model for all the students. It truly is one of the best ways to teach responsibility and self-control to our students.

51. Walk-Talk-And-Regulate—Sometimes getting Billy out of the classroom for just five minutes to "walk-talk-and-regulate" with another staff member will be all he needs to get refocused and back-on task. Offer this as an option when Billy can't seem to settle back down with the resources in the classroom. Physically getting out of one environment for a break with a person Billy can trust into a different environment is needed.

52. Welcome Students—When students enter school or their classrooms, they need to be welcomed every time—every day. Billy needs to feel included. He typically has a history of feeling unwanted, unlovable, and unaccepted. Welcoming students, making eye contact with them, and addressing them by name inherently says, "We are so glad you are here today and a part of our class family, Billy!"

When you are greeting students, be sure to use their name. Dale Carnegie is quoted to have said, "A person's name is the sweetest sound." Saying "Hi" is very different from saying, "Hi, Billy." Getting to know all your students' names at the beginning of the school year needs to be a top priority so you can welcome each by his/her by name.

53. Window of Stress Tolerance—Our Billys already believe they are the "bad" kid and they know they are different. Helping them to understand why they are so quick to react can be an incredibly effective way to help them learn how to do things differently. Teach them about the Window of Stress Tolerance and help them to visually see how their nervous systems are simply tuned-up compared to some of their peers and how they typically live moments away from their breaking point. Help them to see this isn't an excuse for misbehavior; it is a learning tool to see how they can identify ways to expand their windows so they can experience more fun, joy, and success at school and in their lives. Use the Window of Stress Tolerance Worksheet in the Appendix.

Appendix

For the most up-to-date and electronic versions of forms in the Appendix,
visit: www.TheTraumaInformedSchool.com/appendix

STUDENT OF CONCERN FORM

NAME OF STUDENT: _____

GRADE LEVEL: _____

URGENCY:　　　Low　　　　　Medium　　　　　High

REPORTING INFORMATION

Your Name: _____

Your Position: _____

Your Relationship to Student: _____

Your Email Address: _____

Date: _____

ISSUES OF CONCERN FOR STUDENT (CHECK ALL THAT APPLY)

Academic Struggles	General Behavioral Issues
Alcohol Use	Homelessness
Anger Issues	Identity Issues
Anxiety (nervous, tearful, and/or tense)	Illness
Attendance	Injury
Abuse (current)	Isolating from Peers
Abuse (past)	Low Frustration Tolerance
Dating Issues	Lack of Participation
Death of a Family Member	Mental Health Issues
Death of a Friend (student)	Notable Change in Appearance
Death of a Friend (non-student)	Overreaction to Circumstances
Depression or Extreme Sadness	Poor Decision-Making
Destruction of Property	Poor Hygiene
Domestic Violence at Home	Self-Injurious Behaviors
Drug Use	Student/Teacher Relationship Issues
Excessive Absences from Class	Threats to Others/Bullying
Family Issues	Too Many Tardies
Friendship Issues	Witness to an Incident
Gender Identity Issues	Other _____

DESCRIPTION/NARRATIVE

Please provide a detailed description of your concern using detailed, concise and objective language.

Thank you! Please submit this form as soon as possible and return it to the SOC Team Leader.

STUDENT OF CONCERN DOCUMENT

NAME	GRADE	STAFF MEMBER REPORTING THE CONCERN	ISSUE OF CONCERN	ACTION PLAN	PERSON ASSIGNED TO ACTION PLAN	OUTCOME

BEHAVIOR TRACKER FORM

NAME	GRADE	TEACHER	RACE	F/R	SLR PRE	SLR POST	SLSC	SLFS	INFRACTION	CONSEQUENCE	P/G CONTACT	ARREST OR CITATION

F/R: *Free or reduced lunch* | *SLR PRE: Self-identified Level of Regulation when student enters office* | *SLSC: Self-identified Level of social connection* | *P/G: parent/guardian*

SLR POST: Self-identified Level of Regulation at end of office visit | *SLFS: Self-identified Level of physical safety at school*

STRESS INDICATOR FORM (ELEMENTARY)

MAD

HAPPY

SCARED

SAD

GRATEFUL

STRESS INDICATOR FORM (SECONDARY)

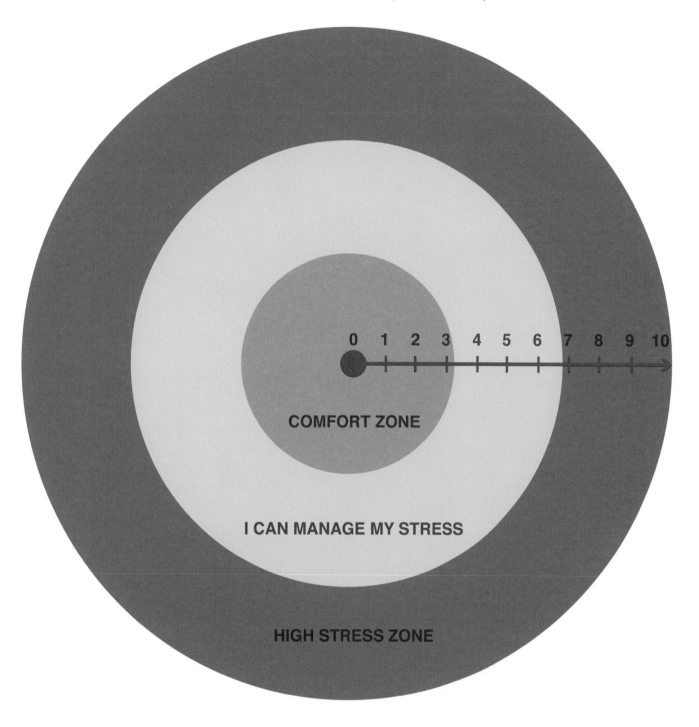

WHICH ONE IS YOUR WINDOW OF STRESS TOLERANCE RIGHT NOW?

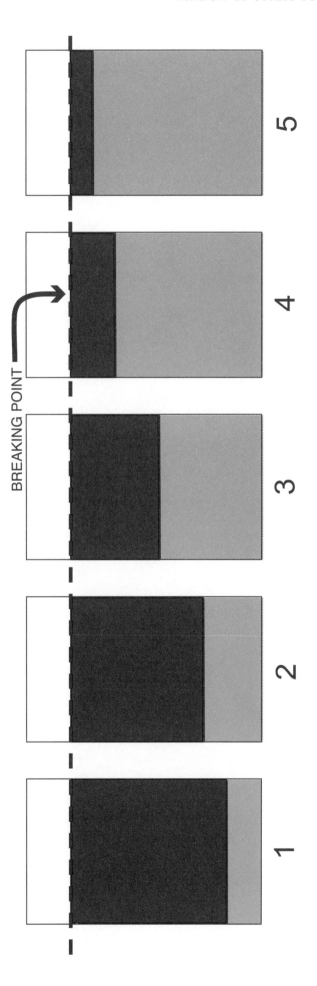

BREAKING POINT

1   2   3   4   5

STAFF ACES SURVEY

☐ CERTIFICATED STAFF   ☐ CLASSIFIED STAFF

SCALE
1 – Strongly Disagree
2 – Somewhat Disagree
3 – Somewhat Agree
4 – Agree
5 – Strongly Agree

Please rank your understanding to the following questions on Adverse Childhood Experience Complex Trauma.

1. I believe that having ACE's can have a significant impact on the life and success of our students if we don't address teaching resilience.

    1   **2**   **3**   **4**   **5**

2. I believe that ACE's impact student learning and behavior in the classroom.

    1   **2**   **3**   **4**   **5**

3. I believe that it is my approach that can make the difference with my students' learning behavior in my classroom.

    1   **2**   **3**   **4**   **5**

4. I believe that my own ACE score affects how I react to my students' behavior.

    1   **2**   **3**   **4**   **5**

5. I believe that my own resilience has impacted my life in a positive way.

    1   **2**   **3**   **4**   **5**

6. I believe resilience can have a positive impact on our students that are impacted by ACE's and Toxic Stress.

    1   **2**   **3**   **4**   **5**

7. I have a solid understanding of ACE's

    1   **2**   **3**   **4**   **5**

8. I learned some new strategies that I am going to try in my classroom to help build resilience in my students through a caring adult relationship.

    1   **2**   **3**   **4**   **5**

9. I feel that the brain research on trauma is the motivator for me to make the necessary changes in my approach with my students.

    1   **2**   **3**   **4**   **5**

10. I believe the more we can connect with our students, the greater chance we have to build their village of support.

    1   **2**   **3**   **4**   **5**

Questions I still have about ACE's and Trauma

Barriers that are getting in my way to move forward with the implementation

Information that I would like Jim Sporleder to cover when he returns

Thank you for taking the time to complete the survey
Your feedback is very important to us!

STUDENT CLIMATE SURVEY

(High School)

Please complete the following survey. No names are used in the survey to protect your identity and confidentiality. You have the option to opt out from taking the survey or to opt out of any questions that you do not feel comfortable answering.

1. Name of your school: _____

2. What is your age? **14   15   16   17   18   19   20**

3. Gender: **Male** ☐   **Female** ☐   **Trans** ☐   **Prefer not to disclose** ☐

4. What is your ethnicity?   **African-American** ☐   **Asian or Pacific Islander** ☐   **Caucasian** ☐

Hispanic ☐   **Native American** ☐   **Other** (please specify) ☐_____

5. What grade are you in?   **9   10   11   12   GED**

6. On average, how would you rate your stress level?

1   2   3   4   5   6   7   8   9   10

(not stressed)   (super stressed)

7. How many years have you been at this school?

Less than 1 year   1   2   3   4   5   5 or more

8. Do you feel safe at school?   **Yes** ☐   **No** ☐

9. What is your favorite part of school? _____
_____

10. What do you wish would CHANGE about school? _____
_____

11. Do you have adults in your life you feel like you can trust?   **Yes** ☐ (If yes, check all that apply)   **No** ☐

Teacher ☐   **School staff member** ☐   **Parent** ☐   **Family member** ☐

Non-family member outside of school ☐   **Other** (please specify) ☐_____

12. Do you feel valued by the staff at school?

13. Since coming to this school, do you feel as though you have become a better student?

Yes ☐   **No** ☐

If yes, please explain what has helped you to become a better student: _____
_____

14. If you were referred to services in the community (such as counseling, shelter, food assistance, drug treatment, doctors, etc.), would you use them?   **Yes** ☐   **No** ☐ (if no, please explain why not)

No transportation ☐   **You don't trust them** ☐   **No time** ☐

Don't know why ☐   **Other** (please specify) ☐

15. What makes this school different than other schools you've attended in the past?

_____

_____

16. What makes teachers at this school different than teachers you've had before?

_____

_____

17. Has your attendance been better since you started attending this school?

Yes ☐   **No** ☐

If yes, why do you think your attendance has improved? _____

_____

18. Do you consider yourself a good kid?   **Yes** ☐   **No** ☐

19. Has your attitude towards school changed since being at this school?

Yes ☐   **No** ☐

If yes, why do you think your attendance has improved? _____

_____

20. If you could make a suggestion for your school to improve, what would you suggest?

Keep things like they are now ☐

I would change the following ☐ _____

_____

_____

FOR A MORE IN-DEPTH AND FULLER VERSION OF THIS SURVEY, PLEASE VISIT:
www.TheTraumaInformedSchool.com/appendix